-6.

The
boo

ALLEN RIDER GUIDES

RIDING OVER JUMPS

ALLEN RIDER GUIDES

Riding Over Jumps

Martin Diggle

Foreword by Joyce Bellamy

J. A. Allen

London

British Library Cataloguing in Publication Data

Diggle, Martin
Riding over jumps
1. Jumping (Horsemanship)
I. Title
798.2'5 SF309.7

ISBN 0-85131-423-6

Published in Great Britain by
J. A. Allen & Company Limited,
1, Lower Grosvenor Place, Buckingham Palace Road,
London, SW1W 0EL

Book production Bill Ireson

Printed in Great Britain by
Butler & Tanner Ltd. Frome & London

Foreword

The majority of weekend riders, especially those who take up riding relatively late in life, tend to find that their riding reaches a 'plateau' round about the level of the B.H.S. Grade II test, and that the pleasures of more varied and interesting activities remain beyond their reach.

Martin Diggle's riding career proves that this ceiling can be passed. His first opportunity to learn to ride came when he was 19, and entered the employment of the Greater London Council, thereby becoming eligible to join that authority's Staff Riding Club, which organised instruction of a good basic level at suitable riding establishments in and around London. Within the next 13 years, he succeeded in passing three of the four B.H.S. Riding Club Grade levels, and his performances on hired horses attained a standard whereby private horse owners became happy to entrust him with the use of their horses for exercise and competition work.

His willingness to ride anything on four legs – from 4-year-old native ponies to ex-racehorses – has endowed him with the ability to strike up a working relationship with horses of all ages and at all stages, and to make the best of their latent abilities. His collection of awards on hired and borrowed horses, ranging from having won his own riding club's one-day event on three separate occasions, to 'external' success in the Open Jumping at the Darent Valley Show, the West Kent Hunter Trials and the Working Hunter class at Halstead, is proof that weekend riders need not be condemned to becoming perpetual spectators to the success of others.

Martin Diggle's practical and down-to-earth text suggests how careful thought and attention to detail can enable 'average' riders to enjoy their riding and competing over fences with safety and comfort to their horses and themselves, by eliminating unnecessary inaccuracies and by developing a positive attitude to their performance.

JOYCE BELLAMY

Contents

List of Illustrations

Acknowledgements

This book could not have been conceived without the instruction, encouragement and assistance I have received with my own riding. I am deeply indebted to a number of people within the riding world, many of whom I am happy to count as personal friends. Although this book is, at times, somewhat critical of instructional standards, I have personally been very fortunate in this respect and where this has not been apparent, the fault has been mine! I would like to express my gratitude to all concerned, and to thank Joyce Bellamy for her Foreword.

This book is dedicated, however, not to a person, but to Mr and Mrs Tostevin's 'Willy', a most brave and generous horse, who gave me some moments I shall always treasure.

MARTIN DIGGLE

Introduction

This book is aimed expressly at novice 'riding club' riders, especially those who do not own a horse. There are thousands of people in this category, many of them keen adult riders from an urban or suburban environment. Such people frequently have no 'horsey' background or connections, and have no real way of evaluating whatever instruction they may receive. There is a definite tendency for the equestrian world to give such people a raw deal, thinking of them at worst as 'Sunday Cowboys', and, all too often, merely as eternal novices who will pay for lessons year after year with no real thought of progress.

These attitudes can do a great disservice to people who, despite restrictions on time and money, have a genuine desire to improve their riding. The problem is compounded by the range of instructional literature available, which tends to polarise into rubbish on the one hand and highly technical books for the advanced rider on the other. There are some good, comprehensible books available, but these are not always easy to seek out, and may still assume a degree of conceptual knowledge in the reader which may not be present at a relatively early stage.

Despite these drawbacks, however, it seems that most keen novices can attain a modest level of competence on the flat in a year or two, depending on time available, degree of perseverance and level of instruction received. A critical period often arises, however, when these riders start jumping, and are all too frequently confronted with clouds of mystique, poor and even dangerous instruction, or possibly both. This phenomenon is widespread, which is a great pity since jumping is something which most riders wish to try at some stage and it is a facet of equitation which should be exhilarating and fun. All too often, jumping is found to be baffling and frustrating. The purpose of this book is, therefore, to give novice riders a clearer idea of what they should expect to achieve in this field, to explode some of the mythology which creates difficulties, and to propose some thoughts and ideas which may help the reader to jump with greater enjoyment and success.

1 First Steps

As already stated, this book is aimed specifically at the novice rider and makes the assumption that the reader is a keen novice, who has spent enough time with a club or riding establishment to have become reasonably competent at riding a well-mannered horse on the flat.

By 'reasonably competent' I mean capable of exercising a fair degree of control at walk, trot and canter, and able to retain balance and control when cantering outdoors; the type of rider, in short, who, if a club member, may have passed the B.H.S. Grade I test and be working towards Grade II.

If you have not reached this stage yet, then you should really be thinking about improving your riding on the flat before doing any jumping; negotiating a jumping course consists largely of controlling the horse on the flat in order to present him at the obstacles, and if you cannot achieve this control then you risk frustration at best and injury at worst. It should be self-evident that riders who are so inexperienced that they cannot guarantee their balance without a tendency to support themselves by the reins should in no way be encouraged to try jumping.

I am pre-supposing that you will be receiving some form of instruction, and that your instructor will be satisfied that you have reached a stage where you can take the first steps in jumping. I am also hoping that you feel sufficiently enthusiastic about it to give it a real go. If this is not the case, do not be ashamed to say so. There is nothing in equitation that will be achieved by an unwilling or uncommitted rider, and a half-hearted approach to jumping is that most likely to result in failure and falls. It is much more sensible to wait until you really want to give it a try than to have a reluctant calamity and be put off.

Preliminaries

Your first steps in jumping are likely to be steps over poles on the ground. You may have already ridden over ground poles in lessons designed to illustrate gaits and rhythm. The main reasons for working over ground poles prior to jumping are, from the rider's point of view:

1) The poles regulate the horse's stride, encourage his interest, and get him thinking about jumping.
2) Especially at walk, horses will stretch their necks and lower their heads when negotiating poles. This helps to illustrate to the rider the need to give a little with the hands in order to retain a soft contact with the horse's mouth, and is a valuable introduction to the concept of the 'following hand', a crucial factor in jumping which we will examine further (in the section headed Rein Contact).
3) In the secondary phase, poles are most helpful in regulating the approach to an actual jump.

The work over poles will initially be at walk, but should soon progress to trot and canter. At this stage, you should be advised to take your stirrups up a couple of holes, which will assist your balance over the poles, and give you an initial feel of riding 'jumping length'. You should not, however, be asked to adopt any fancy positions, neither should you do so voluntarily.

Some riders find the shortened leathers a little strange at first, or even feel less secure, although this should not be the case for those who have enjoyed good free canters when out hacking (when they should have been advised to ride a little shorter than normal). The shorter leathers are, however, necessary when jumping to assist keeping in balance and harmony with the horse, and therefore add to the rider's security rather than detract from it.

2 Jumping

The Horse

It will be helpful to have an idea of what to expect from the horse when riding him over jumps. What will be of most concern is whether the horse is, in fact, able to jump! There has been great debate over the years about whether or not horses jump naturally (actual answer: *some* do), but there is no doubt that virtually all horses, other than the chronically unsound, can be *taught* to jump to some degree. Any animal fit, sound and schooled enough to be used in a reputable riding school should definitely be capable of jumping at least the sort of fences that the novice rider will be tackling, and any school which makes more than the occasional excuse on behalf of its horses should be viewed with suspicion.

Your horse, then, should be up to the job. If you are given a horse which persistently fails to perform, then either the horse should not be in the school, or else you are riding him very badly (which, at this stage, is largely a reflection upon your instructor). If you do have serious problems, ask the instructor to get on the horse and show you how it's done. Assuming that the instructor does get the horse to perform, then you have the chance, by watching and listening, to learn how to cope with the beast. If the horse will not go for the instructor, you should definitely ask for a replacement.

The Jump

Having considered the horse, let us think about what he will actually be doing when jumping. A horse jumps by getting his hocks underneath him, pushing his forehand up with his forelegs, and then propelling himself forward and upward from behind. On the approach, he may lengthen his neck and lower his head, as a 'sizing up' manoeuvre: this will be countered in the lift-off stage of the jump by a shortening of his neck, but as he reaches the top of the jumping parabola, his neck will lengthen again.

Before getting too involved in gymnastic theory, however, we should consider that the act of jumping is really just another transition: the horse is trotting or cantering, and is asked to do something else. When asking for a transition on the flat, the sequence is: prepare – ask – allow. In jumping, this sequence is exactly the same, and all three phases are very important and must be adhered to if you are to enjoy success.

The following points apply to all equestrian movements, but you should consider them very carefully indeed in the context of jumping.

1) If you don't prepare your horse for a movement, he won't be in a position, mentally or physically, to do his best.
2) If you don't ask him, he has no instruction, and any effort he may make will be entirely a result of his own incentive (if any).
3) If you don't allow him to perform, he will quickly decide that he is being taken for a mug, and will stop trying to oblige.

Applying the Aids

PREPARATION Preparing the horse to jump can, in its broadest sense, mean anything that the rider does to influence the horse prior to jumping, and we will look at some of the ideas encompassed by this definition when discussing jumping a course. For the moment, however, we are considering the theory of a single jump in isolation and can define preparation as riding straight towards the jump at an appropriate gait, concentrating on balance, rhythm and impulsion. The most important of these factors, upon which the others are largely dependent, is impulsion, which is not speed, but rather a desire on the horse's part to go forward.

THE AID The fundamental aid to ask a horse to jump is to ask him to continue to go straight forward. If you do this when there is a fence in his path, then he can only obey by jumping. You ask the horse by using your legs; these will, of course, be on the horse at all times, but you will use them to give a distinct aid at the jump just as you would use them to give a distinct aid for a change of gait on the flat. Just as the optimum firmness of aid will vary on the flat from horse to horse and in differing circumstances, so it will over jumps. On a reasonable type of school horse, you should think initially of a couple of squeezes on approach to retain the impulsion, and a light kick at the point of take-off. If your instructor uses ground poles to give you a stride into the fence, this will assist greatly in giving you a feel of the last few strides and the point of take-off.

As you get used to jumping with different types of horses, you will discover that the generous type who really enjoy jumping will need only a light squeeze at a fence, whereas the stodgy, plodding type may need firmer encouragement, perhaps to the extent of a couple of quite strong kicks. Paradoxically, the gassy types often need a strong aid too, since they can get so full of excitement and self-importance on the approach that they need a firm reminder to actually jump when they reach the obstacle.

If you do have to give a horse a real kick at a fence, you must be sure to use only the lower leg (from the knee down), and not be tempted to imitate the small girls at gymkhanas who take the whole length of both legs right off the horse and risk closing them on thin air!

Whatever the circumstances, however, you must remember to give an aid, on any horse and at any jump. If you don't, and the horse doesn't jump, it is your fault.

ALLOWING THE HORSE TO JUMP 'Allowing', in equestrian terms, means rather more than just 'letting'; it also embodies the principles of 'enabling' and 'assisting'. The rider, if he is to be more than a mere passenger, has to do most of the thinking for the partnership, and has also to adapt physically to keep in harmony and balance with the horse. The adaptations in jumping hinge upon two issues – rein contact and the rider's own balance, and we shall now examine the inter-relationship between these factors, and their effect upon jumping.

Rein Contact

This term refers to the contact between the rider's hands and the horse's mouth, via the reins and bit. You will no doubt be aware of this from riding on the flat, and are thus aware of the desirability of maintaining a light, but definite, contact whenever working the horse. You will also be aware, especially from riding at walk where there is a natural movement of the horse's head, that in order to maintain the contact the rider's hands must respond to that movement. As the horse stretches his neck, the hands must 'give' forward, and as the neck shortens, the hands must move gently back just enough to prevent the contact from slackening. The feel in the rider's hands and forearms should be light and supple, with no stiffness or exaggerated, jerky movement.

We have already established that, when a horse jumps, he stretches his neck, but he does so faster, to a greater degree and with less predictability, than at the walk. If the horse is to be allowed to jump correctly and comfortably, the rider must ensure that he keeps the contact light throughout the movement.

The reasons why this is so important are:

1) Hardening the contact represents a crude 'stopping' aid, which will have an adverse effect upon impulsion.
2) Such hardening will make it difficult and uncomfortable for the horse to jump (in severe cases, virtually impossible and actually painful); and a horse who has to drag a rider over fences will quickly lose confidence and enthusiasm.
3) 'Applying the brakes' at a fence can put the horse in two minds about jumping, which is potentially dangerous for both horse and rider.
4) If you *lose* the contact over a jump, the horse will not suffer in flight, but such circumstances frequently occur along with loss of balance, and there is a tendency for the contact to be regained too abruptly, so that the horse gets a tug in the mouth on landing, which he will consider poor reward for doing his duty.
5) On free-going or 'gassy' horses, throwing the contact away over jumps can result in an increasing loss of control from fence to fence, until the rider ends up being carted.

Having established the importance of contact, let us see how attention to balance can help in maintaining it correctly, and also how a desire to keep the correct contact influences the retention of correct balance.

Balance

One of the main attributes of a correct position on the flat is that it keeps the rider in balance with the horse. Since you will have spent much time to date trying to obtain this correct seat, you will be familiar with the basic aspects: a vertical line through head, shoulders, hips and ankles, a deep seat in the saddle and a fairly long length of stirrup leather. As much of a jumping course consists of riding on the flat, it is important that most of the principles which enable one to do so effectively be retained. The 'flat' position, however, pre-supposes that there will be no significant alteration in the horse's outline or balance, and we have established that, in jumping, these changes will occur. It is therefore necessary to find a means of adapting the seat in order to cater for these changes.

The main factors to be considered are:

1) In the first stage of a jump, the horse's centre of gravity will move forwards both as a result of the thrust of take-off and the stretching of head and neck. If the rider is to remain in balance, it follows that he must move *with* the horse. *With* is stressed because it is very important: it should be plain that one cannot stay in balance with anything if one's movements are not synchronised with it, but this fact is frequently ignored by those who teach jumping.
2) The second factor harks back to the question of contact. The rider must allow his hands to travel forward as the horse jumps, and there is a limit to how far they can travel in isolation. Over very small fences, where the horse needs to make little effort, and the stretching of head and neck is limited, a corresponding movement of the hands will be sufficient. When the horse makes a greater effort, however, the rider must be able to respond. In order to do so , he must move his shoulders (to which, of course, the hands are secured via the arms) forward as well. This is achieved by *folding the upper body forward from the hips*, which has the dual function of enabling the rider to remain in balance.

Stirrup Length

In order to facilitate this folding from the hips, it is necessary to shorten the stirrup leathers. This is the adjustment that allows the rider to retain the basis of the 'flat' seat whilst being in a position to adapt to the demands of jumping.

Shortening the leathers has the effect of moving the thigh up and forward, closing the angles at the knee and hip and creating a broader 'platform of balance' for the upper body. It is this platform which makes it easier to fold at the hips without losing balance.

The reader can prove this on horseback, at halt and without stirrups. First, sit upright with a long leg, and try to fold forward from the hips, keeping your back straight and without resting your hands on the horse's neck. You will probably find this difficult, and there will be a tendency for your legs to pivot backwards behind the girth. You will be uncomfortable and unbalanced and are unlikely to feel confident about confronting obstacles in this posture!

Secondly, after reverting to a normal position, draw your knees up high in imitation of a jockey and try once more to fold from the hips. With your thigh 'in front' of you, you should find it very much easier and more comfortable and be able to retain balance and leg position.

These two examples of stirrup length are extremes to prove a point, but having established that too long a leather is going to make jumping very difficult, we can now concentrate on the optimum degree of shortening. For normal jumping, a very short leather is to be avoided, since it makes sitting in the saddle between jumps difficult, and encourages the rider to straighten the leg over fences, pushing the body up and away from the horse.

The ideal length will be that which is short enough to ensure a sufficient platform of balance, without substantially affecting the seat on the flat. Personal physique, conformation of horse and shape of saddle are all factors here, and there is no hard and fast rule. Assuming, however, that you have established a reasonably 'long leg' on the flat, I would suggest that you initially shorten your leathers two or three holes for jumping, on the basis that one hole is too little to be effective and four or more would be, at least initially, rather extreme.

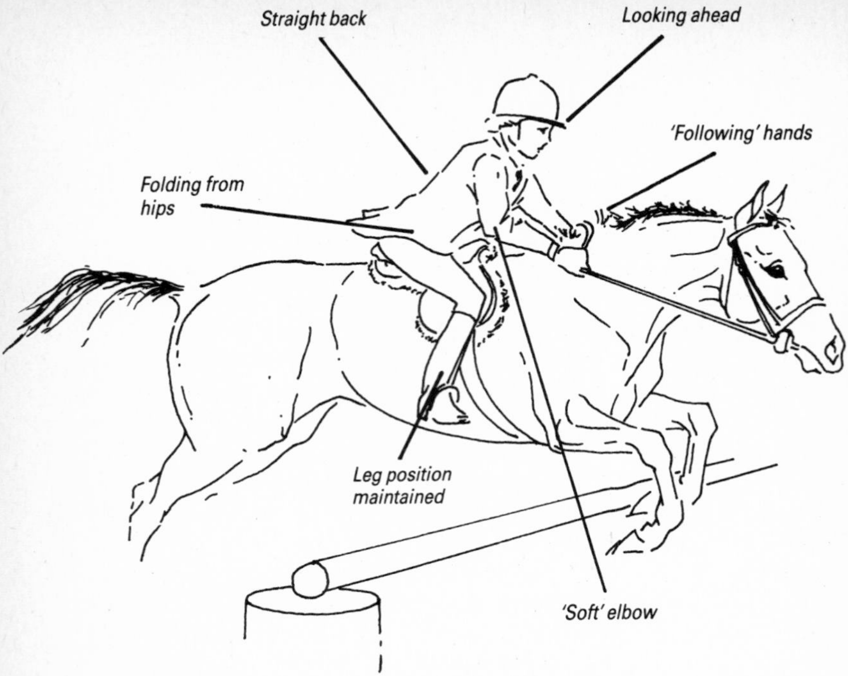

The rider's actions should always be in harmony with the horse, and he should avoid anticipation, delay and extraneous movement. These two illustrations show positions over different jumps. A club member (*above*) jumps a small fence in competition; an international show-jumper (*right*) takes on a large obstacle. Their positions show that they are both adhering to the principles outlined in the text, but the international has folded much more than has the club rider. This is a reflection of the differing effort made by the two horses; the international horse has stretched and rounded almost to a maximum degree; the club horse has merely to 'pop' over the fence. Both riders have made a response appropriate to their horse. It is worth noting, however, that, were the riders transposed, both positions would become incorrect. The club rider's position would become an inadequate response to the effort of the show-jumper's horse, and the show-jumper's position on the club horse would be an unnecessary exaggeration

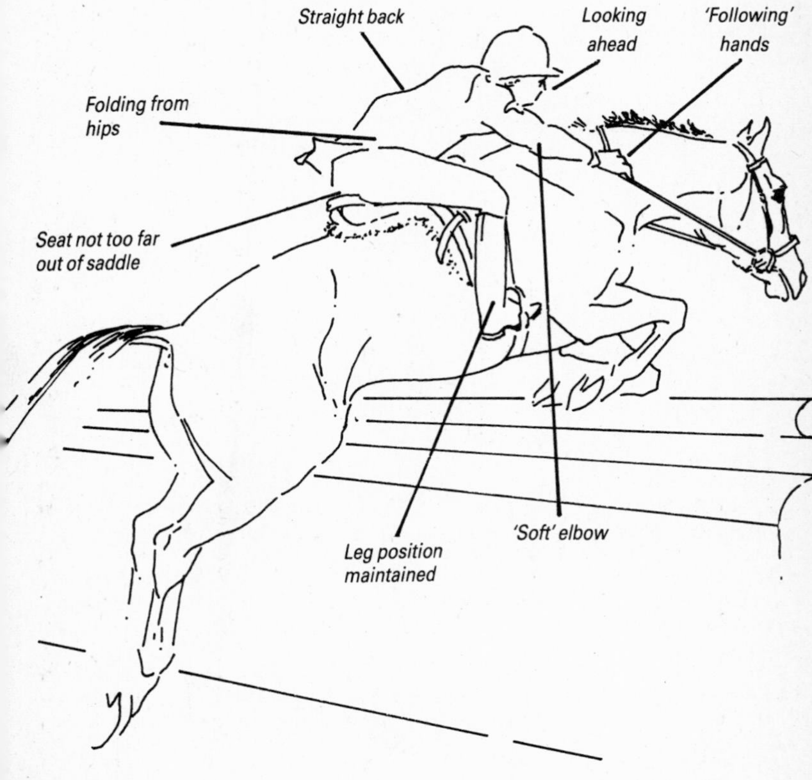
Straight back
Looking ahead
'Following' hands
Folding from hips
Seat not too far out of saddle
'Soft' elbow
Leg position maintained

Putting it Together

If, then, the rider can learn to maintain a light contact and allow the upper body to fold forward in harmony with the hands, he will be able to remain in contact and balance with the horse, and will have the key to successful jumping.

So far, we have concentrated on the take-off and earlier stages of the jump, since these are the most crucial moments. Once the horse has reached the highest point of his jump, the processes reverse; the horse will shorten the outline of head and neck and the force of gravity will overcome the thrust of the jump. If the rider allows his hands and body to continue to react to the horse's movement, everything will revert smoothly to the position adopted prior to take-off. Coming down tends to be easier than going up, and any difficulties or lack of balance at this stage can usually be attributed to errors at take-off. Things to beware of in the latter stages of a jump are either retaining a 'posed' position for too long, or sitting up too early and snatching at the reins. Both of these errors arise from the rider allowing his own misconceptions to override the need to stay in harmony with the horse.

Summary

The rider's position over a jump can be summarised as:

1) The leg remains in the same position throughout – on the girth.
2) The hands follow the horse's movement.
3) The forearms and elbows remain soft and supple.
4) The upper body folds in harmony with the horse's movement.
5) The back remains straight.
6) The rider looks ahead, not down.
7) The seat may come a little out of the saddle in response to the folding body, but not by separate, conscious effort.

3 Getting Out of Trouble

Now that we have examined the things that *should* happen when jumping, we must consider contingencies for the times when things go wrong.

However good a rider may be, there will be times when a jump is met 'all wrong', or when the horse stumbles on landing. In these circumstances, the prime objectives are to keep the horse on his feet, and yourself on the horse, and the best means of achieving these aims are to sit still, keep your leg on and allow the horse to take as much rein as he needs to perform the necessary partnership-saving acrobatics. Riders tackling big 'drop' fences or jumping into water usually take the same precautions, since the circumstances of the jump tend to mimic or induce a similar situation. The practice of 'slipping the reins' is useful in such circumstances.

Slipping the Reins

You should be prepared to slip the reins when: meeting a fence on a bad stride; going too fast; feeling that the horse may hit the fence hard; at most 'drop' fences (fences where the landing side is lower than the take-off); jumping in bad ground; on any occasion when the horse stumbles on landing.

In practice, it consists of opening the fingers sufficiently to allow the reins to run through them in response to the horse stretching his neck. This is in contrast to the normal jumping procedure, where we have seen that the reins are maintained at the same length throughout, with the rider's hands and body following the horse's movement.

Slipping the reins allows the rider to remain in a more upright position than usual, either to create a bracing effect against sudden deceleration, or to counter the effects of a steeper than normal descent. The more upright position will tend to result in the rider getting 'behind the centre of gravity', but although this is not ideal in theory it is acceptable in terms of rider safety. Also, from the horse's viewpoint, it is easier for him to recover with the rider sitting back (but firmly in the saddle) than with the rider sprawling all over his neck.

Effective slipping of the reins requires that the horse is able to 'take' the rein without first getting a pull in the mouth, and the rider's response must, therefore, be immediate once he realises that he cannot, or ought not to, go 'with' the horse. The nearest equivalent action that a rider will take on the flat is when allowing the horse to stretch and take the rein as a reward after working. Although this is usually a much more gradual process than is needed when jumping, familiarity with the feeling will be useful, and it will be worthwhile paying extra attention when carrying out this manoeuvre on the flat.

Another way to practise feel, and to simulate the conditions in which slipping the reins is desirable, is to ride the horse down steep slopes, making no attempt to fold forward, but rather keeping your body vertical to the ground. To do this without hardening the contact it will be necessary to allow the reins to lengthen, as the horse takes enough rein to stretch his neck and balance himself, rather in the manner of taking a drop fence.

The more aware the rider can become of the idea of slipping the reins, and the more adept he can become in practice, the better, since he then has the wherewithal to turn most indifferent approaches into satisfactory jumps. This is not to say, of course, that the rider should not *try* to present the horse correctly at all times, or that he should not, with practise, often be able to guess correctly whether the horse will solve the problem by either 'standing off' the fence or 'fiddling' and react accordingly. Nevertheless, 'slipping the reins' does provide a practical option for the times when the rider is unsure of everything except a desire to get safely to the other side of the fence.

Bill Steinkraus, in his excellent book *Riding and Jumping*, makes the point that 'crude but effective' is not only better than 'crude and ineffective', but is also more useful than 'stylish and ineffective', and this is basically what we are talking about here.

Some instructors take the view that 'getting left behind' (being behind the horse's centre of gravity) is an unforgivable sin, and so do not teach their pupils how to slip the reins, with the result that when the pupils do meet a fence wrong they either give up mentally and allow the horse to stop or run out, or, worse still, fling themselves desperately up the horse's neck. The truth is that, providing a horse is not jumping an obstacle near the limits of his ability, he will usually negotiate it satisfactorily with the rider sitting back somewhat, provided that the rider is sitting still and not pulling him in the teeth. (Anyone who has schooled young or nappy horses over jumps will confirm that, in the early stages, it is virtually obligatory to stay somewhat behind the centre of gravity to get the horse to jump at all.)

Upon landing, you must sit still to allow the horse to recover from whatever error or extra effort he has made, keep your leg on to encourage him to go forward, and only pick the reins up (re-establish normal contact) as the horse recovers. *On no account* should you try to pull a stumbling horse up with the reins – you will only unbalance him more, and possibly even cause him to fall.

Finally, two more thoughts on slipping the reins. Firstly, although useful and sometimes necessary, the practice should not become habitual. If you find yourself doing it almost as a matter of course, you probably either lack confidence in the horse, or aren't feeling when you are correct in your approach and able to go 'with' him. Practising over inviting fences, with ground poles to give you a stride, should assist.

Secondly, slipping the reins has nothing to do with the practice of 'dropping' the horse in front of a jump. This movement, over-popular in the practise arena at local shows, consists of abandoning all pretence of contact in the last stride before take-off, and is frequently accompanied by an apparent attempt on the rider's part to seize the horse's ears. The effect on the horse is to upset him both mentally and physically, and exponents of this fad generally end up by tipping over their horse's head when he decides enough is enough and refuses.

Practise

Some of the principles and techniques already discussed can be practised when not actually jumping. It is a good idea, for example, to practise riding with shortened stirrup leathers, in order to get used to the feel and to control the horse in all gaits on the flat. You should think about sitting 'into' the horse just as if you were riding normal length. Oddly enough, the deeper your seat becomes through flat work, the easier you find it to ride short. This is because, as your seat deepens, it will rely less on any grip from the legs (until it needs none at all) and consequently your stirrup and leg length will have less bearing upon your basic position.

You should also practise folding from the hips, although I do not advocate extended periods of posing round the arena out of control, as seems to be the norm. In practice, the folding movement is only necessary for a couple of seconds at a time at each jump, and we have seen that it is not a set position, but rather a reaction to each jump. What is important is that the folding comes from the hips, with the back straight and the head looking forward, not down. One way to get the feel of this is to think of pushing the stomach down towards the thighs. This can be practised on a horse, or on anything else upon which an approximation of the riding position can be achieved. The other important thing to practise is maintaining the correct degree of contact, and this will be just as important to your flat work as to jumping. Any halfway decent instructor will keep an eye on their pupils' contact, but in 'riding-in' periods or when hacking you can practise lengthening and shortening the reins, and allowing the horse to 'take' the rein, whilst concentrating on the feel and the horse's reaction.

Avoiding Bad Teaching

When one is learning anything, one is dependent, especially in the early stages, upon the advice and instruction being realistic and accurate. With jumping, it is unfortunate that these criteria are sometimes lacking, and I believe that the general standard of jumping instruction available to the novice, non-owner rider is poorer than the flat instruction available to them. Some of the 'tuition' available is, in fact, complete nonsense, and, worse still, very dangerous.

The main, and worst, problem is the common belief that there is a fixed position which the rider can adopt on approach to the fence which will result in a good jump. This fixed position, usually and erroneously called 'the jumping position', is generally taught as an exaggerated and uncomfortable version of the type of position a rider *should* adopt just after take-off in response to the horse's movements. Various justifications are put forward for this teaching: photographs of show-jumpers trying to clear big spread fences off a bad stride are produced (the assumption being that the extreme position adopted by the rider has been established for the last three strides before the fence); or, more bizarre, it is suggested that such a position will give the novice 'confidence'. What happens in fact is that riders unfortunate enough to be taught in this fashion find that the horses they ride frequently run out or refuse, and they themselves spend a lot of time on the floor.

The reasons are:

1) Riders told to adopt these bogus 'jumping positions' are so concerned about what they are supposed to be doing (and finding it so difficult) that they give the horse no instruction or assistance, and thus the horse either chucks it in or else climbs over the fence anyhow, with the rider out of balance.
2) Even if the rider can spare time to think about the horse, he is in no position to bring his influence to bear because he has, by adopting the prescribed position, surrendered the agencies (seat, back and leg position) which would enable him to do so.

To jump successfully, especially in adverse circumstances, it is essential that, during the approach, the rider remains in a strong position, and that position is *in the saddle*. A study of experienced riders will confirm this (watch show-jumpers, or, better still, event riders, approaching tricky combinations). Even steeplechase jockeys, riding as short as they do, will sit on the approach to a fence if they feel they are going to meet it wrong, or their mount is in need of assistance.

Beware then, of the instructor who teaches posed approaches; you can be pretty sure that such teaching is based on theory rather than experience, and that you, as the guinea pig, will be the one to end up with mud on your breeches. Or teeth.

Problems and Errors in the Approach

We are still looking for the moment at a single, straightforward jump, and making the assumption that the horse you are riding is adequately schooled, sound and correctly tacked up. Given these criteria, errors and problems will be mainly rider-related, but we will also consider circumstances where the rider's problems stem from difficulties with the horse, rather than being purely technical errors.

The two main areas where trouble may occur are the approach to, and the actual jumping process at, the fence itself. The former will, of course, have a major impact on the latter, but the converse is also true in that, if a horse is consistently hampered in jumping, he will become more difficult to ride on the approach, being either reluctant to jump or desperate to get it over with. So, let us look more closely at the main problems and errors in the approach.

LACK OF BALANCE Since we are assuming that the horse is well and is adequately schooled, the problem of balance is likely to relate to one of the other factors. Let us examine them in more detail, and consider remedies.

CROOKEDNESS Although fences can certainly be jumped at angles, it will assist the novice rider if he can ensure that at least the last three strides of the approach are ridden 'head on' at the centre of the fence. Since the majority of fences in the school and the show-jumping ring are approached round corners, it is important that the corner is ridden accurately, so that the correct line of approach is achieved. Overshooting the corner is fairly rare, but can be corrected simply by accurate riding. Cutting the corner, on the other hand, is often a case of the rider allowing himself to be dictated to by the horse. If the horse has got a bit keen and has learnt where a jump is, he will often try to hurry into it by cutting the corner, dropping his inside shoulder and becoming unbalanced. This anticipation is just as undesirable as a horse anticipating any other movement and the rider must be ready to ride turns firmly and decisively on the line *he* has chosen. If the horse is allowed to duck round corners, he may well get away with it much of the time, but there will also be times when he will catch himself out, in which case he will usually run out to the same side of the fence as the direction in which he has just turned.

Another cause of crookedness is when a rider tries to 'contain' a keen horse once the partnership is heading straight for the jump. Whilst the desire for full control is very commendable, it is a fact that some horses will seek to evade it by swinging their quarters out to the side (rather like a bicycle having the front brake only applied). When this happens, the rider must ensure that he keeps an even pressure with both legs, and does not try to 'hold the horse up' too long. In the practise ring, this type of horse will often settle if ridden quietly in circles with just the occasional 'pop' over the jump from a short approach. In competition, the rider's best bet is usually to allow the horse to go on fairly freely at the first few fences, which may have the effect of settling him, as this type of behaviour often indicates a highly-strung horse who will calm down once he is allowed to get on with the job.

TOO MUCH SPEED In most circumstances, speed is not a prime requisite for good jumping; it is impulsion which is required. If you watch top show-jumpers in the practise ring, you will see them jump large fences at a steady pace, with only a few strides approach. Despite the lack of pace, however, their horses will be moving with great energy, and with a desire to go forward and jump.

The rider who confuses speed with impulsion will bustle his horse into jumps, losing rhythm and control and getting his horse into a long, flat outline. The longer a horse's stride, the more wrong he can be at a jump, and he will either have to take-off a long way from it, or get in close on a shortening stride and fiddle his way over.

The alternative source of excess speed is, of course, the horse; but before laying too much blame at his door we should remember that it is the rider who is supposed to be in control! We are not, after all, talking about lunatic horses or those fit for three day eventing, but about school horses who are showing a little exuberance at being able to do something other than trot round a school. If these horses want to go, this should be to the rider's advantage, and if he keeps his leg on the horse and rides with a blend of firmness and tact, using half-halts if necessary, he should obtain a good result. The half-halt is an action in which the rider braces his back, closes his legs on the horse, and pushes the horse forward onto a resisting (not pulling) contact. As the horse responds by moving his hocks underneath him, and 'lightening' his forehand, the rider eases the contact, allowing the horse forward before he executes a downward transition. The half-halt is used for collecting/lightening/balancing the horse and to encourage him to 'listen' to the aids.

The two things not to do on such a horse are just to sit there and hope he will take you round, or to try to wrestle him to a standstill.

TOO LITTLE IMPULSION This can be caused on a temporary basis by lack of balance (for example, a poor turn), but the two main reasons are:

1) Sluggishness. Horses given to novice riders to jump should not be too sluggish. However, in practice, most riders find themselves at some stage on the school 'patent safety', which tends to be a large, broad, slow-witted horse whose virtue is that he will not take advantage of anybody, but whose drawback is that his mental processes are matched by his physical actions. To compound the problem, such horses are usually ridden by beginners who, understandably, are in no position to set them about their business. These horses are not usually wilfully stubborn, but are victims of circumstance and physique; they are, nonetheless, rotten rides for jumping, and call for a good deal of patience and work on the part of the rider. It is no good springing things on them suddenly and sharp, short turns are to be avoided. They may offer more impulsion at trot than canter and, if they need waking up by use of the whip, this is better done before the approach to the fence than at the last moment.
2) Underriding. Paradoxically, riders sometimes fail to produce sufficient impulsion in horses which are basically keen. This often occurs on Thoroughbred types, who tend to be either mentally 'switched off' or 'full on'. What happens is that the rider, having found a horse more free-going than desired in the past, gets on with the idea of 'keeping him quiet'. While the principle of keeping the horse calm and obedient is a very good one, it is a mistake to think that this can be achieved by sitting

like a mouse and not doing anything. (Top dressage riders, whose horses appear to go so lightly and freely, do not achieve this state without years of hard work and intensive schooling.)

In correct riding, impulsion is created and controlled; in underriding, no real attempt is made to create impulsion. With a really 'hot' horse, this approach can be very dangerous, since the horse may annexe all control, but with a basically honest horse, his reaction is more likely to be confusion and loss of enthusiasm. He is looking to be sent about his work, but gets no encouragement or direction. Horses so ridden *do* tend to slow down, but the results are not good since, lacking impulsion, they jump poorly, the rider finds it hard to retain his balance and a snowball effect is thereby created which often leads to the horse giving up in disgust.

The cure is with the rider, and it is important to remember that a horse who shows enthusiasm should be encouraged. The points made earlier (too much speed) should be borne in mind, and also the fact that experience will prove that it is easier to jump a horse which offers a little more than necessary than one which doesn't offer enough.

'STOPPING' THE HORSE This is a complete negation of the correct features of jumping and consists of the rider coming into the fence sitting against the horse with a fixed hand, and with no real intention of asking the horse to jump. The only justifiable reason for this is complete loss of confidence on the rider's part; this is something which should not be allowed to happen at a decent establishment. However, it should be noted that this reaction by a rider, however much we may sympathise with the underlying causes, is a recipe for disaster in that it guarantees a bad jump which will do little to restore confidence. The remedy is to go back to the beginning, a point which should be readily understood by a good teacher.

The other possibility in this case is that the loss of confidence is a temporary one brought about by the rider being well and truly 'carted' at the jump. Again, one would hope that this would not occur, since horses which behave like this are fairly rare, and certainly not novice rides. If it does happen, there are two possibilities. The first is to try and circle away from any obstacles and keep circling smaller until control is re-established. The second, for the intrepid, or those who are too close to the fence to pull out, is to sit down and kick like fury on the last couple of strides. This will help concentrate the horse's mind on the jump, and give you your best chance of avoiding the consequences of his galloping straight through it, or stopping dead or ducking out at the last moment. If you just sit there, anything can happen.

'DROPPING' THE HORSE This has been dealt with earlier (Slipping the Reins) and I will merely add that the only justification for completely abandoning the contact is if a rider realises that he is terribly wrong at a fence. If so, his only choice is to keep his leg on, give the horse complete freedom of head and neck and hope that the horse can get the partnership out of trouble. I wonder whether those riders who habitually 'drop' their horse are admitting that they can never get it to a fence on a decent stride?

Problems and Errors at the Fence

The main problems at the fence itself are all negations, in various forms, of the correct procedure, but it is worth considering *why* they constitute faults, in order that the rider can more assiduously try to avoid them. Let us look more closely at them.

GETTING IN FRONT OF THE CENTRE OF GRAVITY This is a cardinal error in jumping, and the most likely to result in injury to the rider. The mistake is invariably made before take-off, since it is very difficult to 'overtake' the horse in flight. It is usually the result of the rider adopting a pseudo-jumping position on the approach. Once 'in front' of the horse, the rider has no control and is entirely reliant upon the horse's actions regarding his future in the saddle. This error is responsible for most of the refusals and unseatings which occur to novices, and also contributes to many run-outs. The cure is not to anticipate the take-off: quite apart from the problems caused to the rider, the horse's task is not made any easier by having an unbalanced weight sprawl onto his forehand just as he is about to elevate it.

GETTING BEHIND THE CENTRE OF GRAVITY As we have seen (Slipping the Reins) provided it is done for a good reason, and the reins *are* slipped, this may not constitute a fault at all (although it may still indicate a fault in the approach). If, however, the rider regularly resorts to this tactic over straightforward fences, then there is an indication that either he is riding too defensively, or else he is still lacking co-ordination. In both instances, work down a jumping lane on an honest horse should bring about improvement, but exhortations to 'get forward' in isolation are likely to prove counter-productive.

NOT SLIPPING THE REINS The real crime, and it is a very serious one, is for a rider to sit back and *not* slip the reins, relying on the horse's mouth to drag him over the jump. Apart from the considerable discomfort that this will cause the horse, it is also dangerous for the rider in that the horse, while jumping, will be unbalanced and distracted and will jump in bad style. It is therefore essential that the rider who habitually sits back, or who feels that he is likely to at a particular fence, is prepared to slip the reins the moment the degree of contact increases.

RUNNING THE HANDS UP THE MANE This fault is common in those riding 'hot' horses, or others who are reluctant to ride with a reasonable length of rein for fear of losing control. Having approached the jump with a very short rein, the rider can only avoid hardening the contact by thrusting his hands forward up the horse's mane (riders in such circumstances being most reluctant to slip the reins). As a result of this manoeuvre, the rider can get perilously far out of the saddle and, if the horse stumbles on landing, there is a real risk of being pulled over his head (this happens quite a lot to novice race-riders). The remedy is for the rider to practise controlling the horse on the flat on a longer rein; it is a fact that 'hot' horses often respond to a little tact and subtlety, whereas riding them on a very short rein just winds them up more as they seek to escape the hard contact.

HANDS 'PLANTED' ON THE WITHERS This is a very common fault. Instead of the hands being kept free to respond to the horse's movement, they are pushed into the withers on take-off, thus establishing a length of rein which is inflexible for the duration of the jump. If the horse requires more rein, he will just get a pull in the mouth and possibly unbalance the rider. If the rein is too long on take-off, then contact will be lost on landing; the horse may take advantage of this by speeding up or, in a combination fence, ducking out of the second element.

Planting the hands often occurs in riders whose instructors place too much emphasis on 'going forward'. The rider finds himself getting too far forward and plants the hands to retain balance. Similarly, riders who have got into the habit of standing in the stirrups often plant the hands for the same reason.

HANDS IN THE AIR It is not unknown for riders to raise their hands on take-off. Although a reason sometimes given for this is that the rider thinks such action will assist the horse, this is pretty hard to believe. The only reasons which have any logical credence are:

1) That the rider is unable to retain any semblance of balance on take-off, and just tips backwards. This suggests that the rider is too inexperienced to be attempting jumping, or is riding an unsuitable horse over unsuitable fences.
2) That the rider is trying too hard to drive the horse forward with the seat alone, so that the upper body gets behind the vertical, dragging the hands and arms up and back. This is not unusual, and the cure is for the rider to think more about leg aids and the desirability of being in a position from which folding from the hips can be achieved (practise on a free-going horse can help).

STANDING IN THE STIRRUPS This is a result of misconception. Either the rider believes that he is somehow helping the horse, or else he has a vague notion that he should 'get out of the saddle' over the jump. The overall effect is to lock the knee and ankle joints, straighten the leg, point the toes down, get the backside a long way out of the saddle, look down instead of forward and plant the hands on the horse's withers. Apart from being of no assistance to the horse, this position is *very* precarious for the rider, and should be remedied before a fall results. The rider must concentrate upon retaining the leg positon with flexed knees, and think of folding his upper body from the hips rather than springing vertically into the air like a jack-in-the-box.

LOOKING DOWN This is often connected with standing in the stirrups and rounding the back rather than folding. It is also associated with a generally 'defensive' attitude, or it can be sheer habit. It is a fault which should be attended to, not only because of the association with other positional errors, but also on the basis that the rider tends to go where he is looking!

Especially when it is related to riding defensively, or to habit, an effective cure is for the rider to approach the fence a little more strongly, with his gaze fixed on an object at eye-level on the far side of the fence. If the object in question is the instructor, waving money or making rude gestures, the improvement may be dramatic.

The other type of looking down occurs when the rider has got into the habit of leaning in exaggerated fashion to one side or the other of the horse's neck. This may be understandable in people who have been hit in the face by a horse jumping hollow-backed and throwing its head up, but this is fairly rare and would hopefully not happen with horses given to novice riders. I believe that, in most cases, it is a copied fad; it is best avoided as it tends to have an unbalancing effect upon both horse and rider.

GENERAL STIFFNESS With a lot of jumps made by novice riders, there is no serious error, but a general stiffness in the rider results in some degree of discomfort to themselves and/or the horse. Since balance and contact are affected by stiffness the jump is, therefore, less than perfect. This problem is only natural at first, since the process of jumping correctly does call for a good deal of dynamic balance and, like many other things, it takes a while to establish 'feel'. The rider can, however, hasten the path to improvement by avoiding any tendency to brace himself, stiffen, or pose at the jump, concentrating instead upon being positive, fluid and supple. In the rider's 'defence', it has to be added that it is much easier to correct errors of technique on an honest, sensible and even-striding horse.

Errors After the Jump

It may seem strange to suggest that an error can be made after the jump is completed, but, looking ahead to the process of jumping a course of fences, it will become apparent that there is an inter-relationship of obstacles, and that the first few strides after one fence become the first few strides of approach to the next. Therefore, even when practising over a single jump, the rider should endeavour to avoid any bad habits which could affect his riding of a following obstacle.

The main errors are:

1) Losing impulsion after a fence.
2) Letting the horse run on.
3) Allowing the horse to duck round to the back of the ride.
4) Looking back.

The first three faults are symptomatic of the rider 'packing up' after the jump – the feeling being 'I'm over, that's it'. This attitude must be eradicated if the rider is to jump courses effectively. (It is significant that, even at an advanced level, it is often the fence *after* a problem fence which causes problems, because riders are so glad to get the bogey fence out of the way that they relax at the next, and ride it poorly.) Therefore, once a jump is completed, the rider should promptly but smoothly regain any contact or balance lost and seek to re-establish the rhythm of the approach. The horse should neither be allowed to 'die' nor to rush off round the school, and should certainly not be permitted to duck off at an angle in search of his friends. The rider should proceed away from the fence in a straight line at the gait from which the fence was approached, riding a smooth downward transition before negotiating any tight turn or approaching other people on the ride. At a later stage, these comments will apply equally to a rider in the practise ring prior to an event.

The remaining fault, looking back, is a tempting habit, but since it is totally pointless and counter-productive, it should be eradicated as soon as possible. It is not unnatural to look round if you have hit a fence; but, if the fence is still standing it is a waste of effort and, if it has fallen, staring at it will not make the poles leap back into their cups. Furthermore, if the rider turns his head, he will almost certainly turn his shoulders and hips as well, thus detracting from his position and unbalancing the horse. Also, he will not be looking where he is going and may lose the line to the next fence. This is a lesson which the rider who faults at fence 'B' whilst confirming that he has not faulted at fence 'A' will not readily forget.

4 Types of Fence

So far, we have been talking mainly about 'the fence' from a theoretical point of view on the assumption that the fences jumped in the initial stages will be straightforward and inviting.

Now, however, we must consider the various types of fence to be encountered at club or local level show-jumping, hunter trials and one day events. With course-builders being increasingly influenced by the major events, the rider must expect to be confronted with miniature versions of almost anything.

Despite the huge diversity of individual design there are still really only two fundamental types of fence, the upright and the spread.

The Upright

An upright fence is, as the name suggests, a fence which has vertical height but no significant width, examples being planks, poles in a single plane, post and rails and, for practical purposes, most walls and thin hedges.

The Spread

Spread fences are more diverse and range from the familiar triple bars, oxers and parallels of the show-jumping arena to open water and ditches, with an almost infinite variety in between.

The Fan

A crossbreed of the upright and spread is the fan fence. This is constructed with a single wing one side and two or more on the

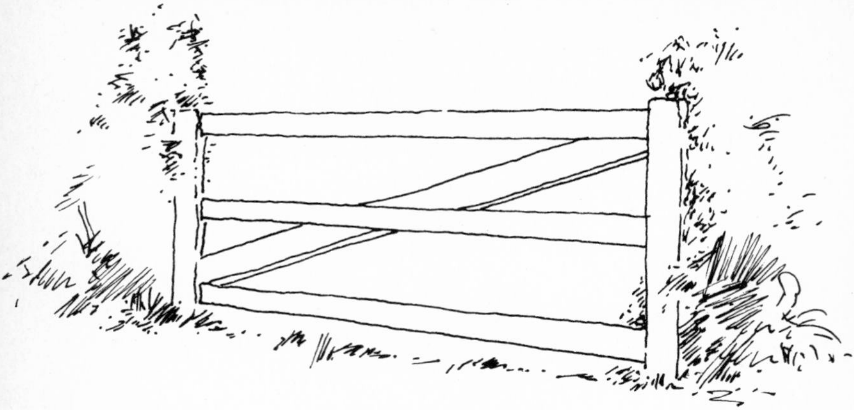

Typical upright fence

Spread fence

A crossbreed of the upright and the spread – the fan

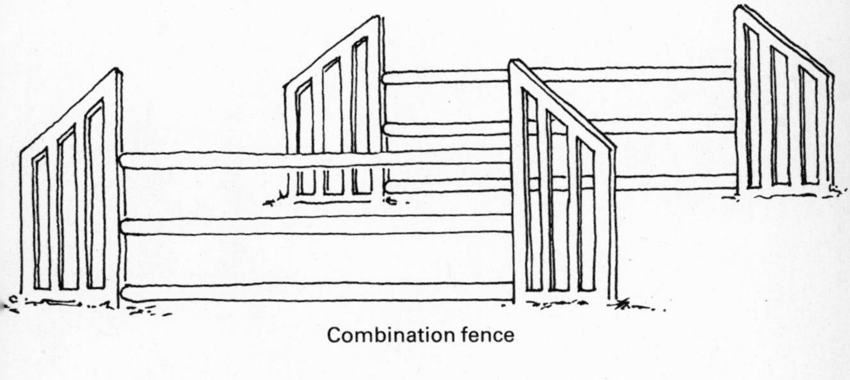

Combination fence

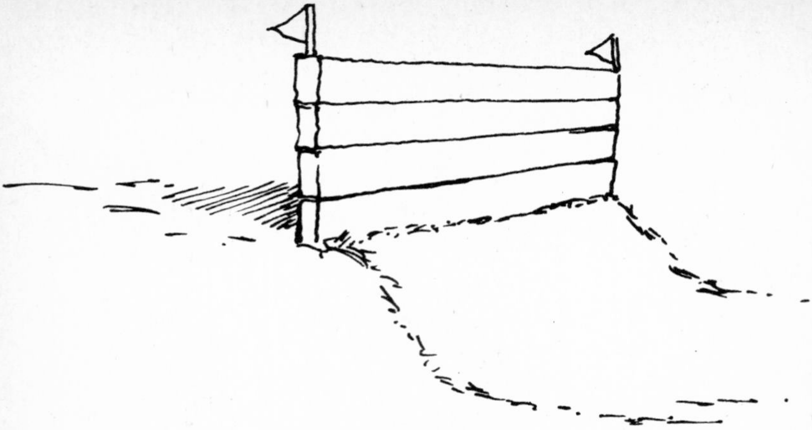

Using the lie of the land – the drop fence

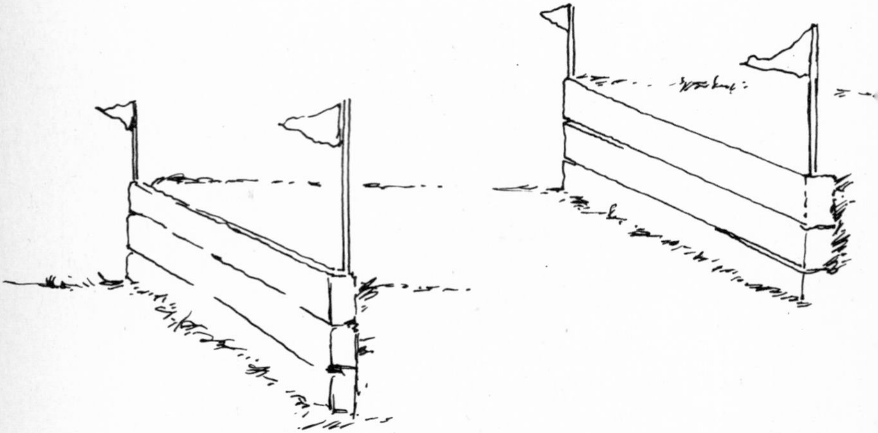

Typical step fence

other side, with a series of poles arranged in a fan effect so that one side of the obstacle offers a relatively high, virtually upright fence, whilst the other side offers a lower jump with a relatively wide spread. Unless there is a good reason to do otherwise, a jump in the middle of the fence will split the difference between the two factors, but, if the rider chooses to take the jump at either end, he will effectively be riding either a spread or an upright.

With each type of fence, the course-builder can add further dimensions with other features such as:

COMBINATIONS These are obstacles at which more than one jumping effort is required, for example, 'bounce' fences, doubles and trebles. A 'bounce' is an obstacle where the horse is required to jump the first element and then take-off again over a second without putting in a stride. Such fences are not normally found in the show-jumping arena, but are becoming increasingly common in cross-country events. Doubles and trebles consist of two and three elements respectively, but allow for one or two strides between each. In show-jumping, a double or treble is treated as a single obstacle; if, for instance, a horse refuses at the last part of a treble, the whole thing must be attempted afresh, but in cross-country competitions the rider can opt to re-present the horse at the 'problem' element only.

DROPS Drop fences are those where the landing side is appreciably lower than the take-off, and usually occur where a cross-country course-builder has utilised the natural lie of the land.

STEPS These have gained popularity through the influence of eventing and proper steps are purpose built of packed earth with wooden facings, each step having a 'tread' depth of about 2·7m (9ft). The horse is required to 'bounce' up or down a series of two or three steps. At a more advanced level, the steps may be incorporated into the approach of an obstacle, but at novice level a couple of small steps will often constitute the whole thing. Sometimes, a natural change in land level may be doctored to produce a single step rather than used to site a drop fence.

5 Assessment of Fences

Having looked, then, at the main categories of fences which may be encountered once the rider starts attempting courses, we should look next at factors which tend to influence how easy or difficult an obstacle will be to negotiate. Before analysing these factors, there are two points which should be made:

1) Subject to the assumption that the horse is operating well within the limits of his natural ability, height is not a very important factor as far as he is concerned; he will jump a 1 m (3·2 ft) fence which he considers 'easy' by other criteria much better than a 0·7 m (2·5 ft) fence which he considers 'difficult'.
2) Nonetheless, riders do not always see fences in the same light as horses. Therefore, instructors should never cajole a rider into attempting a fence which the rider considers will 'overface' him. The reasons are obvious:
   a) However 'easy' a horse may indicate a fence is to jump, poor riding stemming from apprehension can change this, with serious consequences for both horse and rider.
   b) Both with schooling horses to jump, and training riders, the foundation stone is confidence; the needs of the individual have to be considered, rather than adherence to some rigid formula, in order that progress may be made.

Therefore, although we are now going to look ahead to what the rider can expect to come across in time, in the early stages of jumping courses the instructor, or a responsible organiser, should ensure that riders are jumping straightforward fences on horses which are as accommodating as possible.

What, then, makes a fence 'easy' or 'difficult'? Since it is the horse who does the actual jumping, most of the factors relate directly to his viewpoint.

Visibility

In every aspect of equitation, it is important that the horse knows what is required of him. In jumping, it follows that the sooner he can get a clear view of an obstacle which he can appreciate is a jump, the better his chances of jumping it. It is by no means rare for horses who have habitually jumped one type of obstacle to have initial problems when confronted by another type, simply because they do not associate it with the act of jumping. Whilst it is unlikely that the novice rider will have to deal with such a case, it is still worthwhile learning the lesson that the horse must understand what is being asked of him.

Since horses have rather strange vision and little imagination, they usually find solid, obvious fences the easiest to jump. Such fences as walls, fallen trees and constructions of telegraph poles may seem daunting to the rider at first sight, but they are meat and drink to the average horse, who will negotiate them with far more zest than a flimsy, airy construction which he can barely see.

The other aspect of visibility is that which is influenced by actual light conditions; a fence in heavy shade, especially if jumped out of bright sunlight, can cause problems for both horse and rider, whereas a fence jumped from relative darkness into the light will usually prove attractive unless it is some over-gaudy construction which actually acts as a mirror.

Groundline

The groundline is the base of the fence where it meets the ground, and it is from this point that the horse measures his take-off. A fence which does not possess a groundline (for example, a single pole suspended between wings) can still be jumped, but the horse will find it relatively difficult since he will have to guess his take-off point. If a show-jump is constructed in long grass, it makes sense for the groundline pole to actually be a few centimetres off the ground so that it is not hidden by the grass and its purpose negated, but this procedure is often beyond the wit of some course-builders.

A groundline which is a little nearer to the line of approach than the highest point of the fence will encourage good jumping

X=nearest practical take-off point.

A horse measures his take-off zone from the groundline. The take-off zone is the area in front of the fence from which the horse can be expected to jump cleanly, and is usually reckoned to be a distance from the highest part of the fence of 1 to 1½ times the height. 1½ times is considered the norm by course-builders constructing combination fences. If the horse gets nearer to a fence than its vertical height, he risks hitting it 'in front'. Over small jumps, the take-off zone will be wider, since the horse can get away with taking off further from the fence, but as height increases, so does the need for accuracy.
The illustrations show: (above) *groundline at base of vertical fence; 'normal' take-off zone established;* (centre) *groundline brought forward. Take-off zone measured from groundline now somewhat further from the fence, promoting a more 'scopey' jump. Also, the horse can now get rather* nearer *to the fence than the take-off zone indicated, and still be 1×vertical height from it, and jump cleanly;* (below) *false groundline, tending to draw the horse too close to the jump*

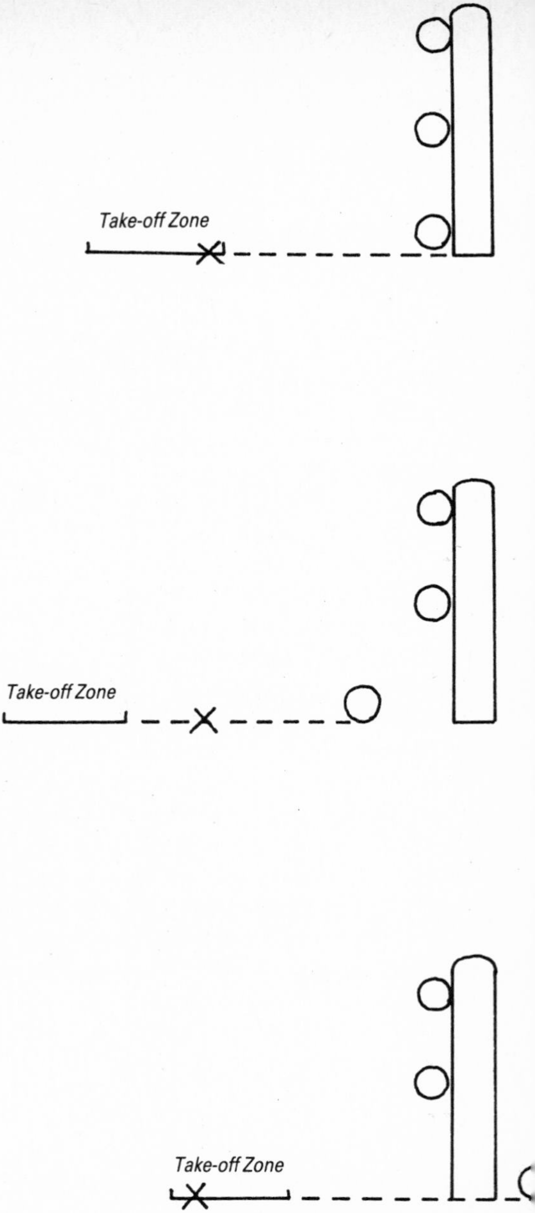

The geometry of groundlines

since it will give the horse a better perspective of the fence and cause him to make a slightly greater effort. Also, if he comes in on a bad stride and 'fiddles', such a fence will give him a little more room, and make him less likely to hit it with his forelegs than an upright fence would. The explanation of this is simple geometry: if the groundline is 0·3 m (1 ft) closer to the line of approach than is the highest point of the fence, then the horse has a little extra room in which to elevate. If the high point of the fence is directly above the groundline, then there is no extra room. Therefore, fences which slope gently away from the approach tend to be relatively easy; not only are they inviting to the eye, but they actually give more margin for error.

A false groundline is one which is further from the line of approach than a line drawn vertically down from a higher part of the jump (for instance, the gently sloping fence jumped from the opposite direction). Such a fence is very difficult for a horse, who will tend to assume that the high point of the fence is vertically above the groundline and thus take off too near the fence. Fences with false groundlines have no place in novice jumping, and are seldom seen in any competitions, although they may occur naturally. There is, however, a type of fence which may produce a false groundline by optical confusion, and that is a single pole fence situated a short distance from the start of a downslope. In some circumstances, it seems that the horse may see the brow of the slope beneath the fence, and initially size up the jump using this point as the groundline. I recall watching a hunter trial where an apparently innocuous fence sited in this fashion caused a large number of abrupt refusals from horses who had been going very well up to that point. Most jumped the fence at the second attempt from a short approach, and I can only assume that they were caught out on first sight. For this reason, I would suggest that any similar obstacle should be approached steadily and with extra care.

Width

The wider a fence is between the wings (or marker flags), the easier it should be to jump. The reasons are straightforward:
1) A wide fence always looks lower than a narrow one of the same

height and this will make it appear more inviting, at least for the rider.

2) With a narrow fence, a poor, crooked approach can easily produce a run-out, whereas with a wide fence the rider is quite likely to get away with it as long as there is some vestige of impulsion. (Which is not to say that you shouldn't try to ride every approach as well as possible.)
3) A wide fence gives a choice of approach. You do not have to jump it in the middle, but can take into consideration such factors as best line of approach, best line to the next fence and ground conditions. If the ground is very wet and likely to cut up, it can be useful to establish the likely popular approach to such a fence and plan to jump it in a different spot. If your horse must, perforce, jump most of the course out of a sticky morass created by other competitors, you may as well give him a break where you can.

Approach

We have already seen that the manner in which a fence is approached is the most significant factor in the success or failure of the jump. On a course, especially across country, the rider must be aware of the physical geography of the approach, and be ready to adapt his technique as circumstances dictate. The factors to bear in mind are:

GOING Good level ground with a little 'give' in it is ideal from the horse's point of view, whereas deep mud, hard, rutted ground or slick grass over a hard topsoil can all create difficulties. Jumping out of heavy going requires considerable effort (try it yourself), and the rider should concentrate upon keeping the horse moving strongly forward between leg and hand, but should avoid 'chasing' him into a long, flat outline. Rutted or slick ground should be treated with caution, and the rider should try to be as quiet and sympathetic as possible and avoid fiddling around with the horse, which can cause serious loss of balance in such circumstances.

LINE OF APPROACH A fence in plain sight which can be approached direct is going to be easier for both horse and rider to size up than one which is approached down a winding path through dense woodland. With the latter, the rider should ensure that he knows exactly where the fence is and approach as steadily as possible in order to avoid springing a surprise on the horse.

Especially in show-jumping, there are times when the horse may be confused as to which fence he is aiming at. This may sound almost crass, but show-jumping courses are often both compact and complex; it is not unusual to ride a turn with the intention of jumping a fence across the diagonal of the arena and finding that the horse's attention is caught by another obstacle which appears to be more obviously in front of him. Good course-walking, which prepares the rider to prepare the horse, will ensure that, in such circumstances, the rider is spared the embarrassment of being taken over the wrong fence by his keen but uninformed steed.

ANGLE OF APPROACH This may be on the level, uphill or downhill. Level approaches are the 'norm', where the horse will be using his natural length of stride, but uphill approaches, provided they are not extreme, can prove at least as easy to ride, since the horse's stride will be shorter (meaning he can be less 'wrong') and he will also be using his hocks actively to propel himself up the gradient. Downhill approaches are the hard ones, since the horse will tend to be going long and flat, with his hocks out behind him. Furthermore, the landing will be steeper than usual and there will be less horse in front of the rider. Downhill fences must be treated with discretion (although not trepidation), and it is a good idea to establish a steady rhythm before starting the descent. Small, narrow fences may be best negotiated from trot, with the rider allowing canter, if offered, on the last couple of strides, but not before.

'Special' Fences

Under this heading I group the following:

DITCHES AND WATER Obstacles consisting of, or including, ditches should always be treated with great respect, since most horses have an instinctive distrust of holes in the ground, probably resulting from race memory of sabre-toothed nasties. Even bold horses, who have learnt to sail over familiar ditches at home, may have a very long look at a new one and the rider should always be prepared for this reaction, especially on an unfamiliar mount. Small, shallow ditches on the take-off or landing side of solid, eye-catching fences usually pose the least problem, but deep, gaping ditches in plain view beneath a fence are among the most difficult obstacles to jump. The best plan of attack is to approach such fences in a strong but controlled fashion, driving on hard for the last few strides. The rider must give the horse all the encouragement and assistance he can, but should still be prepared for the possibility of the horse slowing into the fence and jumping 'big'. For this reason, a ditch is an exceptionally bad fence to approach with the rider 'anticipating' the jump.

Water jumps, in general, cause fewer problems than ditches (the average horse will probably jump a water-filled ditch better than the same ditch dry), but the same criteria apply. However, water jumps do not always consist of jumps over water, they may require jumps into it. At novice level, this is unlikely to involve more than popping over a small log into a few centimetres of water, but nonetheless it is important to know the principles involved. The first of these is to jump into water slowly, since it exerts a considerable 'braking' effect; the faster the horse enters, the more deceleration he experiences, with unbalancing results. The slow entry should, however, still be an impulsion-filled one; the horse should not 'die' on the edge and fall in anyhow. The second principle is that, because of the steeper-than-usual angle of approach, and the braking effect of the water, it is almost obligatory for the rider to slip the reins to some extent, and he should be sensitive to the horse's requirements in this respect.

COMBINATIONS We have already dealt with these briefly but, in assessing them in more detail, it is worth looking at the technical theory behind their design. In novice events, bounce fences invariably consist only of two elements; trebles, which are fairly rare, should not consist of just a single stride between elements (which is very demanding on the horse and rider), but should have at least a two stride gap somewhere in their construction.

In order to assess and negotiate such fences properly, the rider must be able to identify the striding. Although this is not difficult, it is alarming how many people are unable to do so.

In textbooks typical distances are often quoted for combinations. The 'classic' distance for one non-jumping stride is 7·4 m (24 ft), a two-stride distance is generally given as 10·15 m–10·77 m (33–35 ft), and a bounce distance as 3·7–4·6 m (12–15 ft). These figures are, however, calculated on the basis of large, forward-moving horses negotiating sizeable jumps, and the distances given would be too long for the average school horse of limited scope. More appropriate distances for novice courses would be approximately:

Between 5·54 and 6·46 m (18 and 21 ft) for a one-stride distance
Between 8·6 and 9·54 m (28 and 31 ft) for a two-stride distance
Between 3·08 and 3·7 m (10 and 12 ft) for a bounce.

The differences between these distances should be immediately apparent to the eye, but it is always a good idea to pace out combinations in order to establish whether they are likely to ride 'short' or 'long', and it is worthwhile practising taking 1 m (3·2 ft) strides to this end. It should also be borne in mind that there are legitimate reasons for combinations to vary in distance, these being:

1) Actual size of the elements (as above).
2) Composition of elements. Horses generally cover more distance in the air over a spread fence than over an upright of the same height. Therefore the total distance in a combination of spreads will normally be greater than for a similar combination of uprights.
3) Ground conditions. In heavy going, combinations should be shortened somewhat.
4) Approach. Combinations taken uphill should be a little shorter than normal, to allow for the shortened stride of the horse. Those taken downhill should normally be a little longer, although the course-builder should be discreet if hard or slick ground is likely to cause horses to 'prop' or shorten.
5) Course-builders' discretion. Novice riders should never be faced with trick distances, but a course-builder may put in something a little short to see who's awake, or to limit the size of the jump-off field.

ANGLED COMBINATIONS Normally restricted to the cross-

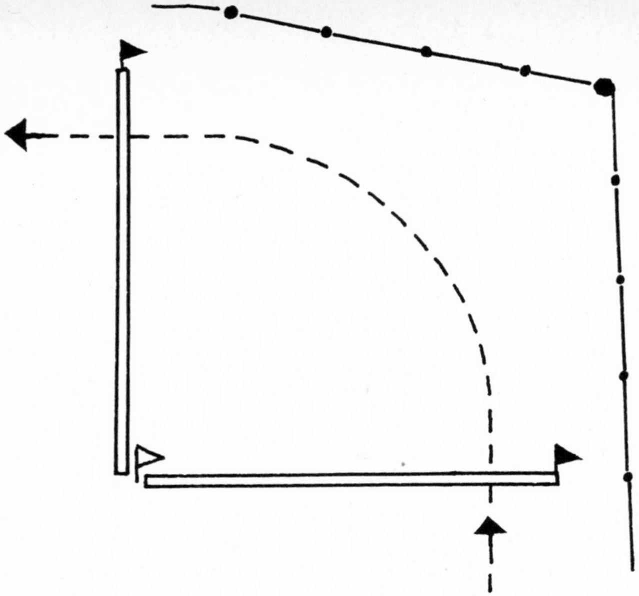

Typical pen fence, showing preferred line through

country course, these are obstacles in which the elements are not parallel to each other, the main types being pens and Vee fences.

Pens are usually located in the corner of a field, with the two jumping elements forming adjacent sides of a box, at an angle of 90 degrees. Space is at a premium (there is usually room for no more than a couple of strides, and they may have to be on a bend), and a steady, controlled approach is called for, with active riding between elements. It usually makes sense to make as much room as possible by jumping both elements at the appropriate end, rather than in the middle.

Vee fences are so called because of their shape. They may offer a variety of lines of approach, so that they can be jumped as a bounce, a single stride double, or even a two stride double. Some also offer the option of jumping a corner in one leap, but this is not recommended at the novice stage since a run-out is the best to be hoped for if things go wrong.

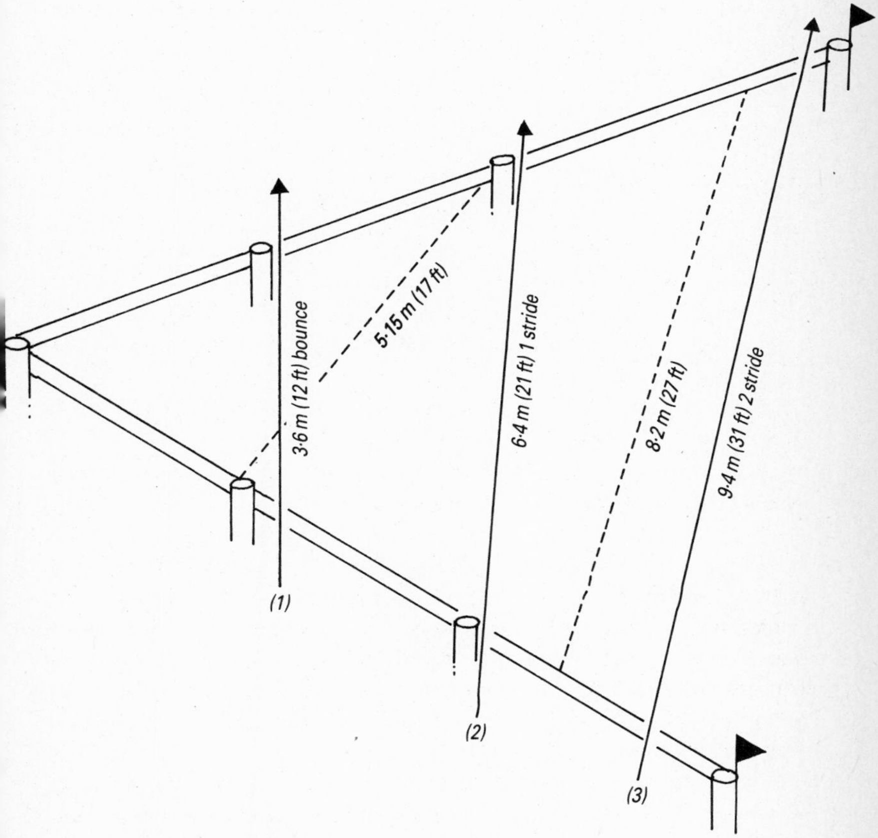

Routes through a Vee fence: (1) fast, although demanding accuracy and impulsion; (2) straightforward, with some 'room for manouevre'; (3) plenty of room, but flirting with run-out possibilities at the second element. The dotted lines indicate two 'wrong stride' routes to avoid

With these jumps, the most important thing is to decide which line you wish to take; establish a physical point you can use as a 'sight', and ensure that you ride your approach accurately along the chosen line. Vee fences are often of post and rail construction and the upright posts may make a very good sighting line. But, if you do use them for this purpose, you should ensure that you are not led by a combination of attractive stride and sight line into jumping one or both elements at a foolhardy angle.

All combination fences need to be ridden decisively, with the final element uppermost in the rider's mind; it is no good flopping in over the first part and then grinding to a halt or allowing the horse to run round the second element. This remark is especially applicable to trebles, which require extra mental and physical effort from both horse and rider. Furthermore, trebles require to be approached very straight, since a small deviation from the correct line at the first element will be magnified greatly by the time the final element is reached.

Angled combinations, by definition, make it practically impossible to approach all the elements head on; the straighter one element is approached, the more acute is the angle created to the next. With these fences, it is usually best to split the difference and jump each element at a slight angle, thus avoiding extremes.

Siting of fences

Before leaving the assessment of fences, there are some further aspects of siting to be considered. The first of these also involves construction. A fence may exist in isolation in an open space (when it is known as an 'island fence'), or it may be bounded on one side by a solid feature (wall, hedge, etc.) which acts as a wing, or it may be part of an existing natural obstacle (for example, a flagged portion of a field boundary fence).

Show-jumping courses usually consist entirely of 'island' fences, although there are times when a solid boundary exists to one side of a show-jump, thus moving it into the second category. Examples of this would include jumps in an indoor arena where the jump cups are mounted in brackets fixed to the wall of the school.

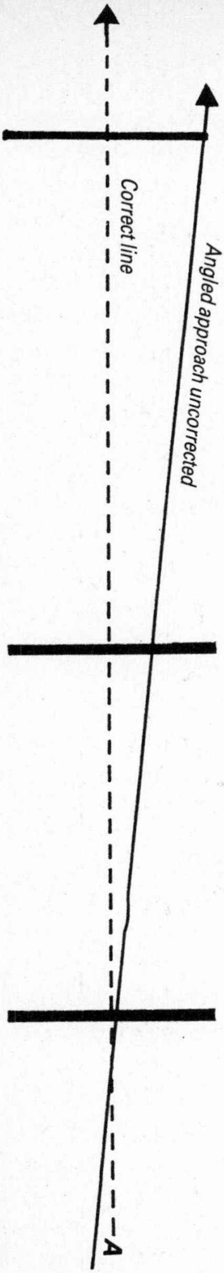

How not to jump a treble (*left*). Note how slight the initial angle of deviation (A) is

The Vee fence (*below*) showing the best line (solid) and the most risky lines (dotted). The most likely 'run-out' spots are marked X

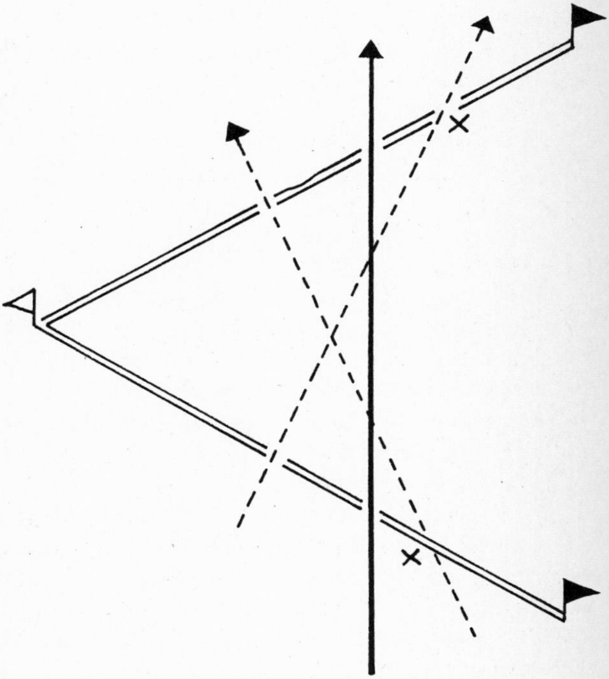

On cross-country courses, 'island' fences should, ideally, be rare, since the principle is to make as much use as possible of natural features, which would generally fall into the second and third categories. In practice, however, one is likely to encounter all three types of jump on most cross-country courses.

In general, an 'island' fence is more difficult to jump than the other types, simply because it will be relatively narrow across the face and because there is a possibility of its being evaded to either side. A fence which has a solid boundary on one side is a rather easier proposition, since the rider can be sure that his horse cannot run out in that direction and will be unlikely to even consider doing so. With such fences, it makes sense to jump them towards the side which is 'sealed off', so that if the horse does take a dislike to the obstacle it will be harder for him to run round it.

A fence which is bounded on both sides by something at least as big and solid as itself is the easiest from the rider's point of view; although it is still possible for the horse to refuse, it is impractical for him to attempt a run-out. If such a fence is substantially smaller and more inviting than its natural 'wings', it is a real gift, but this should not prevent the rider from riding it properly.

There is one other element in siting considerations which is probably the most quirky and unpredictable, but which can, nevertheless, have a profound effect. This is the magnetic attraction that home, the horsebox, or his friends, can have on your steed. Most horses find these influences attractive to some degree (which is why kind course-builders design show-jumping courses with the first fence jumped towards the collecting ring), but there are some animals who have developed such a fixation that they go like dead donkeys away from the attraction only to metamorphose into Grand National candidates the moment they turn round. It goes without saying that a pre-knowledge of such foibles is almost essential if such horses are to be kept under control.

Notwithstanding these extremes, however, the 'attraction factor' should always be borne in mind when assessing fences; the first fence of many cross-country courses, for instance, is jumped away from the attractions and, however inviting it may seem, such a fence should be ridden into firmly. On a more subtle plane, many courses swing past box parks, stables or fields populated by other horses, and all can have a distracting influence. It is worth remembering that no fence is easy if your horse is looking, or napping, away from it.

6 Walking the Course

Walking the course, whether prior to show-jumping, horse trials, or hunter trials is essential if you are seriously intending to ride your best. The object is not merely to gain a vague notion of where the jumps are, but rather to establish a detailed and decisive plan both of the actual track you intend to take and of how you will deal with any problems posed by the obstacles themselves. After walking the course you should have a similar mental picture of your intentions as you would prior to riding a dressage or Prix Caprilli test.

If you were to ask a top show-jumper about a course he had just walked, he would be able to tell you the distances through the combinations almost to within a few centimetres, and the number of strides between all the fences built on 'related' distances; similarly, you will find that top horse trials riders will walk the entire cross-country phase three or four times before tackling it. Whilst I am not suggesting that a novice rider should go to these lengths, there is a lesson to be learnt; if the top riders feel a need for this degree of reconnaissance, then surely the ordinary rider needs to take the matter seriously. What, then, is the procedure for walking a course?

Firstly, it is helpful to have a general idea of the way round before starting off, since you will then be able to concentrate on the more crucial aspects of the task rather than wandering aimlessly about looking for the next fence. Any well-run cross-country competition will have a diagram of the course on display, and it is worth having a preliminary look at this, or even making a rough copy by which to navigate. Show-jumping courses sometimes have a plan on display as well but, failing this, it is a good idea to stand in the middle of the arena and work out the basic route from the fence numbers prior to actually walking the track.

The second thing to do is note where the start is, especially in relation to the first fence. This may sound stupifyingly obvious, but think for a moment. Although, in cross-country competitions, the start will be a 'standing' one, will this entail riding directly away from other horses, or is the line to the first fence past the distractions of stables, boxes or collecting ring? Furthermore, is the first fence in plain view, or will you have to negotiate a turn to it? How far from the start is it? All of these questions will require some response when you are riding the course, so you must be aware of them beforehand. In show-jumping, the location of the start can be even more crucial. Sometimes, at indoor courses where room is at a premium, it can be quite physically difficult to even get to the start! The normal procedure in show-jumping is that, shortly after the rider has entered the arena, a bell will be sounded, after which the rider has 60 seconds to commence the round. This preliminary period, both before and after the bell, can be used to 'warm up', and establish the desired rhythm and gait, and it is here that the position of the start becomes critical, because once you have gone through it, whatever your intentions, you will be deemed to have commenced your round. Also, the location of the start, and the route to the first fence, should have a major influence upon where, and upon which rein, you ride your warm up.

If, for instance, the start has to be approached round a turn on the left rein, it is logical to establish canter on that rein in a part of the arena from which you can flow smoothly on to the start. There is no point in riding in on the other rein, or in a part of the arena from which you cannot readily commence the round.

Once you have decided how best to get through the start and over the first fence, course-walking takes on a more generalised aspect. The fundamental question is: 'What is the most appropriate route to the next fence, bearing in mind how I intend to jump it?' To answer this question, you will have to apply the criteria described earlier (Assessment of Fences), and consider any other factors you feel relevant. Sometimes, one aspect of a jump may suggest one approach, whilst another factor may suggest something different. With so many variations and permutations possible, there can be no hard-and-fast rules here, and commonsense tempered with experience will produce the soundest judgements. The one rule that *does* apply is this: if a fence has you in a quandary, stay with it until you have made your best decision about how to tackle it, and stick with this decision. What you must avoid is coming to actually jump the fence with no idea about how to do so. If you are unable to decide what to do for the best, resolve to ride for the middle in a strong, but controlled fashion. Horses, being simple creatures, often do not see complications (which may be, at least partially, in the rider's imagination) and will usually respond to a blend of plenty of encouragement and no hindrance by finding their own route over obstacles which have the rider's brain tied up in knots. Note, however, that this is *not* an exhortation to 'leave it to the horse', but rather a definite plan to take the straightforward route and give the horse every encouragement.

There are two other considerations in course-walking which are likely to be more relevant to show-jumping than cross-country. The first of these is the problem of two fences built at a slight angle to each other, with only four or five strides between them. This does not present a major difficulty, but can be a 'catch out' if you are not alert, since the angle will be just sufficient to produce a run-out (or, more probably, steer-out). The answer is to be aware of the angle, and to resolve to get onto the straight approach to the second fence as soon as possible after jumping the first, rather than charge on regardless and end up wrestling the horse into the second fence at an acute angle.

The second consideration is to be aware of changes of rein and the effect they can have. From riding on the flat, you will be aware of the desirability of cantering with the horse's correct leg leading and the effect that an incorrect lead can have on balance and bend. Frankly, when you come to ride the course, you may well find yourself too concerned with absolute fundamentals (staying on, wishing your friend hadn't brought the camera, etc.) to remember which leg you are on. So, make a prior note of places where changes should occur and this will at least prepare you for the possibility of the horse becoming unbalanced at these junctures. If this does happen when you are tackling the course, your memory should be jogged sufficiently for you either to ride a half-halt and give the horse a chance of changing legs himself, or, if time and space permit, coming back to trot and asking for the correct lead.

This is not, I hasten to add, the complete formula for 'flying changes' for international show-jumpers, but it is a practical way of giving your horse a chance and is a good deal better than bashing on regardless. With experience, you will become more aware of the horse's balance, and circumstances which may affect it, and the use of the half-halt as a means of remedying loss of balance.

The very last thing to think about when course-walking is the position of the finish. You have not completed the course until you have crossed the finishing line with the partnership intact; I have known several instances of riders being so relieved to get over the last fence that they have ignored this final necessity. If the finish is near, and in line with, another fence, be sure that you plan to steer round the obstacle after finishing, because if you jump an extra fence, whether intentionally or not, you are likely to be eliminated.

7 Riding-in

This is the process of warming up yourself and your horse prior to taking part in a competition. At club or local level all too often time, facilities and space are scarce, and you should ensure that you make the best possible use of whatever facilities are available. This is important enough on a horse with which you are familiar; if you are riding a strange horse, it is absolutely essential.

The basics of riding-in are much as they would be at the start of a lesson. You should check that the tack is correctly adjusted, and that your stirrup leathers are an appropriate length for jumping. Once you have got an initial feel of the horse at walk, you should do a little work in trot and canter, at which stage you can start asking yourself questions about your mount: Is he keen and active, or sluggish, is he giving more attention to the show atmosphere than to you, is he 'on the forehand' or does he go hollow-backed, will he bend through the corners? And so on.

Although you will not be in a position to attempt in-depth re-schooling, you should still try to improve the horse's way of going as far as practical, and where this relates mainly to his mental attitude, you should expect a fair degree of success. The keen horse should be nurtured (he is looking forward to the job, which should help you), but if the keenness overflows into excitement, you will have to work for a calmer attitude, riding in walk, steady rising trot and circling and changing rein. The sluggish horse will have to be woken up (I repeat, a horse cannot do anything properly without a reasonable degree of impulsion, let alone jump). It is worth remembering that a couple of sharp smacks with the whip at the first signs of non-cooperation can often set a horse about his business, whereas he may be quite happy to ignore an hour of incessant tickles. (I am still assuming that you are not being asked to ride a lame, sick or unfit animal.) If the horse is still hard work – the riding school brontosaurus – then you will have to resign yourself to working hard; remember that such horses often go relatively better in trot than canter. What you must not do is give up and stand around in the practise arena wishing you had taken up croquet: you can learn something from riding any horse, and at least the bad ones make the average ones seem easier.

The horse who is looking around rather than concentrating needs to be gently persuaded that listening to you can be just as much fun, and you should seek to attract his attention by asking for plenty of transitions and changes of direction. If he is a persistent sightseer you can give him a few nudges with your lower leg to remind him that there's someone on top, but you should remember that a horse like this is, at least, alert, and is likely to perform well if you can get him on your wavelength.

If the horse has marked physical problems, you are unlikely to be able to do much about them in the space of a few minutes, but you should be able to establish an idea of how best to compensate. The horse who is 'on the forehand' will seek to use your hands as a fifth leg, leaning on you and giving you a 'heavy' feel. You should avoid the common error of thinking that such a horse is trying to take a strong hold, and thus shortening up the reins, because you will probably find that he just stops. The best method of getting a reasonable short term result from this type of horse is to ride with a good length of rein and a fairly light contact, and keep trying to drive the horse's back end underneath him. A horse who moves in this manner finds it quite difficult to jump in good style, because he has to do more work in order to elevate his forehand and gives himself little assistance from behind; furthermore, he will tend to pitch forward on landing. Despite these difficulties, however, a horse who goes on his forehand may perform surprisingly well over fences within his compass as long as he enjoys jumping. The rider's best bet is to avoid trying anything fiddly on the approach to the jumps and to concentrate on riding forwards quite strongly, remembering that it is fairly hard to see a good stride on such horses, and concentrating on the principle of keeping the leg on and waiting.

The hollow-backed horse poses many problems, especially if the condition is pronounced. It is physically difficult for such a horse to either start or stop easily and correctly, and he will invariably jump in poor style, making it hard for the rider to retain correct contact and balance. Such horses come into the category of 'not novice rides', but you will probably encounter one sooner or later. If the condition is not strictly related to back problems, but arises from mouth trouble (previous ham-fisted riding, dislike of bit, or teething trouble), you may be able to improve matters by keeping a very light contact and encouraging the horse to move his hocks underneath him by riding plenty of circles. If the horse does bring his head down and bend his neck, he should be encouraged to go in the improved outline with plenty of leg aids and a soft hand. While he is going hollow, however, you should avoid giving him too much rein, since if a horse does 'take off' with you while he has his head in the air he will not be easy to stop.

Horses which will not bend laterally may be suffering from bad skeletal conformation and/or bad schooling, or they may be going badly by way of evasion. In the first instance, it is unlikely that you will be able to establish much improvement quickly, but, whatever the cause of the problem, you should still *try* to get the horse moving a little better. Riding turns and serpentines at walk and sitting trot may help; you should encourage the horse to look round the turns by opening the inside rein (not pulling back on it) and giving firm and obvious leg aids.

Unless the horse was purely evading you, and now starts to bend correctly, you will have to bear in mind the need to go as wide as possible on your turns once you start the course, otherwise you run the risk of coming into jumps going virtually sideways.

Reverting from this harrowing catalogue of difficulties, let us assume that your horse is a straightforward ride, or that you have managed to smooth out any basic kinks on the flat. Once you are reasonably satisfied with his performance at walk, trot and canter, you can move on to the business of practise jumps. The idea of practise jumps is not to prove that you can jump a single pole a foot higher than anything on the course, nor is it to scare yourself silly when you find you can't. It is simply to get the horse thinking about jumping, and going smoothly over a straightforward fence, and to accustom yourself to the feel he gives you.

If the show is well-organised, there should be a couple of

practise fences available; a very low, easy 'first-go' fence and another which should be a straightforward equivalent to the sort of thing you will meet on the course. (If there is only one fence, and it is being used by people who have built it in a fashion unsuitable for you, you will have to wait your chance to rebuild it suitably. Do not be tempted to practise over an obstacle which varies markedly from your requirements, nor in circumstances where you are likely to be hustled, crowded or ridden into.)

Your first two practise jumps should be over the smaller fence and are mainly an introduction for the horse. You should approach from trot, giving yourself plenty of room and your horse a chance to see the fence, and ask for canter (with a correct aid) a few strides from the obstacle. Do not be surprised if the horse does not jump particularly fluently at the first attempt; many horses, including good ones, benefit from a 'sighting shot'. You should learn much more from the second attempt, which should follow straight on with the same approach. Hopefully, the horse will have got the message and will jump more freely and in better style. If he gets excited and wants to run at the fence, you will know that the rest of the practise session will entail discreet riding, with lots of circling around fences, jumping only when the horse is calm and listening to you. If, on the other hand, he remains sluggish and unimpressed by proceedings, now is the time to chase him over (or, if necessary, through) the jump, because if you are going to get round the course you must get some response in the practise arena.

Providing you obtain a satisfactory jump from your horse, you can now take the opportunity to find out more about his style of jumping, and what manner of approach suits him best. You can attempt the larger practise fence, and you should jump from both directions if possible. (Practise fences should normally be jumpable on either rein, but you have to take care not to collide with someone else coming the other way!) You should vary your approach, coming from trot and cantering the last few strides, coming from cantering large round the ring (if the horse is going smoothly and obediently) and coming on a fairly short approach off a circle, to simulate jumping a fence off a corner. You should not, however, try anything too tricky or clever, because your aim is to build mutual confidence, not destroy it. Furthermore, there is no point in endless repetition; once the horse has given a satisfactory response to a question, be content. If you try something which does not work, go back to another approach which has produced a better result. Should you have the good fortune to be on a keen, willing and able horse, you need only be thinking in terms of six or eight practise jumps (which will be mainly for your benefit) and, even if you have problems, you should avoid trying to solve them by endless unsatisfactory jumping attempts. Keeping things 'low and simple' will stand you in better stead than the popular error of 'practising refusals'. However the horse is going, try to end your riding-in on a good, or relatively good note, and try (not easy) to time things so that you can proceed directly to the collecting ring and your round. There is no point in having yourself and your horse all primed and ready and then finding you have to wait around for half an hour. If this happens, due to delays on the course, etc., keep gently 'warmed up' rather than hanging around and going to sleep.

Finally, on your way to the collecting ring, remember to check your girth and, if necessary, remind yourself that horses often go better in the heat of competition than they do in practise.

3 Riding the Course

This is the culmination of your course-walking and riding-in. If you have done both thoroughly, all you have to do is put your ideas into action. This is, of course, easier to say than do, but it is a fundamental truth that if you have prepared properly you will be in a vastly better position than if you have not.

Before your first few events, you will probably feel like a diluted jellyfish and wish that your camera-toting friends and relatives would fall down a deep hole. These feelings, which are not confined to equestrian jumping, will quickly vanish once you start your round; you may find yourself surprised by how much of a thrill you experience jumping fences in 'hot blood'. The most important thing to remember is to ride your horse forward and have a real try; you will then have no cause for self-recrimination whatever happens. It is also worth noting, and a credit to equestrian sport, that no experienced onlookers worth their salt are going to laugh at you if things go wrong – these people have almost certainly had similar problems themselves at some stage and their attitude is likely to be sympathetic encouragement. Since the techniques of riding show-jumping and cross-country courses vary in some respects, it may prove useful to examine them separately.

Show-jumping

Upon entering the arena, you should trot your horse round between the fences to accustom him to the arena, and to the idea that he is about to jump. You are not, however, permitted to stand still in front of a fence and 'show' it to the horse. Shortly after you have entered, a signal (buzzer or bell) will sound, indicating that you can start your round if ready, and that you have to start it within 60 seconds. You should remember that you must not ride through the start before the signal is given (if the rules are being applied strictly, you will be eliminated), but once you ride through it after the signal, you are deemed to have commenced your round.

Once the start signal is given, then, you should canter your 'warm up' circle in the place you decided upon when walking the course. Providing the horse is moving well, there is no point in delaying your progress to the start, but if you are not satisfied you should use some time to try and improve him (the 60 seconds is longer than you think). When you go through the start, however well the horse is going, you should be prepared to 'switch him on' a little going to the first fence, so that he knows he is being asked to perform 'for real'. This may merely require a little nudge with the legs and a squeeze on the rein, or you may need to give a kick and a growl of 'go on'. It is usually good policy to ride the first fence somewhat more strongly than the fence would appear to merit of itself, merely because it *is* the first.

Having negotiated the first fence successfully, you should be on your way, and it is now a question of following your planned route and applying the basics, remembering that show-jumping is 'flatwork with fences' and riding with accuracy and plenty of impulsion. If things go wrong round a turn in the heat of the moment, you should try to feel where the horse's quarters are and get them lined up straight at the fence. This is more important than concentrating on aiming the horse's head at the fence, since it is the quarters which provide the power and thrust for jumping; a horse can be looking at a jump with his head and neck, but if the 'engine' isn't lined up behind them, he won't be able to get over.

For the rest of the round, ride the course you have walked. Ride the horse forward and do not assume anything, don't 'anticipate the fences', and don't let the horse dictate to you, however well you think he is going. Think about *balance* where changes of rein occur. Ride the last element of any combination and do not look back.

Whatever happens, keep trying. And don't forget to go through the finish!

After completing the round, remember to bring the horse

gently back to walk before leaving the arena (and give him a pat). If you complete the round in less than full control, you *must* re-establish it before leaving the arena. It is very bad manners, and extremely dangerous, to go charging into a crowded collecting ring.

If you have the good fortune to ride a clear round and find yourself in a timed jump-off you should not, in the early stages, attempt to do anything other than repeat your performance of the first round. Going faster, turning shorter and jumping at angles are skills you will acquire with practise and experience, but if you try for too much too soon, you will probably just end up learning lessons the hard way. In any case, at true novice level, two clear rounds is often good enough for a rosette, although the satisfaction of having achieved them should be sufficient reward in itself.

Cross-Country

Whilst the basic principles outlined for show-jumping also apply for cross-country, there are differences between the two disciplines. The method of starting varies and the greater distance between obstacles, overall length of course and varied terrain of a cross-country course lend themselves to a rather different style of riding.

The start of a cross-country event is usually a 'standing' one. There is a small arena ('box') behind the start into which you will be called a minute or so before your starting time. There should be enough room in the box for you to walk or trot the horse in, and you should do this rather than stand around losing the horse's attention. The starter will usually give you a 'ten second' call before counting you down to start; although you are not allowed to cross the start line before the starter says 'Go', you may time your approach from within the box so that the horse is moving forwards when he reaches the start. Alternatively, the starter may say 'Go when you're ready', in which case you should still ensure that the horse is going forwards when you cross the line: allowing him to stand stock-still for half a minute and then giving him a sudden boot in the ribs is not conducive to a good start.

Once under way, you will need to get the horse into a good

rhythm promptly and it is here that the difference in style compared to show-jumping becomes apparent. If we equate show-jumping to 'flatwork with jumps', then cross-country is basically 'a good free canter with jumps'. Rhythm and control are still priorities, but you can allow the horse to move with a longer stride and body outline than you would desire for show-jumping. Most horses have their own 'cruising speed' which they can maintain without need for urging on or undue restraint and this is what you should aim for. A cross-country course can seem an awful long way round if you are driving on a reluctant horse, or fighting an over-excited one. Furthermore, if the horse is 'cruising' for most of the time, it will be easier for you to gain his attention when riding approaches, and the whole process will be much pleasanter and easier for him.

Hopefully, by the time you come to ride in cross-country competitions, you will be familiar with the feel you get from a keen but well-mannered horse cantering freely; a steady 'pumping' of the horse into your hands, with an offer to quicken on request, but not fighting for his head. On such a horse, you can readily come a little out of the saddle, folding slightly forward as though going over a small jump, and remaining in balance over the horse's centre of gravity by keeping your leg on the girth. This is the position you should be seeking between fences: if the horse needs pushing on, or you have to go into trot, you can revert to a normal position in the saddle, and if he starts to get stronger than you wish, you can remain out of the saddle, but drop your weight back so that you can 'hold' the horse with the big muscles of your legs and back, rather than with your hands and arms. You may also have to change your position somewhat if you hit very deep, muddy going, which will slow the horse down and tend to affect his action. In such circumstances you should sit slightly behind the centre of gravity for your own safety in case the horse stumbles badly, and also give him more rein so that he can use his head and neck to balance himself.

When you reach what you judge to be the approach zone for each fence, you will have to ensure that you gain the horse's full attention. You must remember that, although he may be enjoying a good canter, *he* hasn't walked the course, and he will not necessarily be sufficiently alert to jump a strange obstacle sprung on him without warning. To gain his attention, you should return to a sitting position in the saddle, so that you are in a position to apply all the aids, and give the horse a squeeze between leg and hand. You should then be in a position to ride your approach in the manner you decided upon when walking the course.

Exactly how you approach any fence will depend upon your assessment of the factors involved, but certain principles apply:

RIDE STRONGLY If you consider the fence generally difficult (imposing, 'spooky', etc.), but best jumped from canter, you should get full control of the horse in good time, and ride strongly at the obstacle, bearing in mind that strongly means measured and determined, but not flat-out and panic-stricken.

ESTABLISH THE GAIT If the fence requires that you jump it from trot or walk, then you should establish the chosen gait before the obstacle, and meet it going forward in that gait. You should avoid approaching any fence still trying to 'slow down', since this will only relay negative messages to the horse and result in a refusal or very poor jump.

PREPARE If the fence is straightforward and inviting, and your horse has been jumping well, you can prepare the horse a few strides away (he may prepare himself, pricking his ears at the fence and tending to quicken into it); keep your aids light, saving the 'full steam ahead' aids for any problem fences. However light the aids though, you *must* give the horse some indication that he is required to jump: cross-country courses are littered with riders who thought 'this is one for the photographer' only seconds before landing face first in a ditch.

A further difference between show-jumping and cross-country is that, in the latter, it is quite usual to have more than one rider on the course at a time, the riders being started at set intervals. These intervals should be sufficient to avoid 'snarl ups', but if one rider has problems, or is just much slower than another, he may well be caught. The basic etiquette of this situation is that the rider coming from behind has right of way, and if he catches another between fences, he should merely shout 'excuse me' and pass. The same right of way principle pertains at fences, but discretion and commonsense are called for if accidents are to be avoided. If the fence has a wide face, it is quite in order for both riders to jump it together, but the basic onus is on the rider being overtaken to get out of the way. If he realises he is being caught as he nears the approach zone, he should pull out and allow the following rider past, and if he has had a refusal, he should certainly not clutter up the jump having another attempt until his pursuer has passed. Having said this, it should be stressed that 'right of way' is no justification for galloping straight into a fellow competitor!

When you have completed the course, there should be room for you to ease down gently, without risking collision with other horses, and without having to 'pull up' abruptly. This latter is to be avoided, especially if the horse is tired or the ground bad, because of the risk of tendon, or other, injury. The horse will also require more attention than he would after a round of show-jumping: it will at least be necessary to slacken the girth and walk him round on a long rein until his breathing is normal and he has cooled down. If he is very hot and tired, he should be dismounted, swiftly untacked and led in hand with an anti-sweat sheet on until he has recovered, and is cool and dry.

9 Problems on the Course

There are, of course, any number of problems but for our purposes we will itemise the crucial ones. They are:

Hitting Fences

Knocking a fence down whilst show-jumping will earn 4 faults, whilst a single refusal will earn only 3. Nevertheless, at novice level, a knockdown may well indicate less of a rider error than a refusal. Furthermore, at this level, penalties tend to accrue more from refusals than knockdowns. The reason for this is that the horses are jumping well within the limits of their ability, and can get away with jumping off a fairly poor approach either by 'standing off' or 'fiddling' the fence, still jumping it cleanly. If, however, they are very badly presented at a jump, they are much more likely to stop or run round it than to make a kamikaze attempt. This can be quite comforting to the rider tackling solid fences across country.

If, therefore, you have the odd pole down when show-jumping, you should not worry unduly, but try to analyse any error on your part and avoid repeating it. Only if a normally clean jumper has a succession of fences down should you be deeply concerned, because this indicates serious rider error, most probably either allowing the horse to rush at the jumps and flatten, or else interfering with its mouth during the jump.

The other reason for a horse hitting a fence is, of course, sheer carelessness on the horse's part. Some horses get quite *blasé* about 'knockdown' obstacles (although they tend to treat solid ones with more respect) and there may be times when you are sure that you have presented the horse correctly, only to find that he kicks a pole off. This is something about which you can do very little in the course of a round, since the problem can only be resolved by remedial schooling, which is a matter (and not always a simple one) for an experienced rider. You can, however, console yourself with the thought 'at least it wasn't me that time'.

Refusals and Run-outs

These are the two different means by which a horse can evade tackling a fence. With a refusal, the horse stops in front of the jump, whereas with a run-out he tries to avoid it altogether by going round it. Both forms of evasion are penalised to the same degree in competition.

Leaving aside other causes such as illness/lameness of horse, lack of schooling, 'overfacing', incorrect tack, etc., the causes of both are:

MUTUAL MISUNDERSTANDING This is a fairly rare cause and tends to happen more to established partnerships. Horse and rider both come to the fence with good intentions, but these intentions do not correspond, or, alternatively, both think that the other has got things sorted out. A refusal/run-out in these circumstances does not really constitute disobedience on the horse's part, but rather confusion, and there is little to do but grin ruefully and have another go. Providing the rider is positive, the horse will usually jump without fuss on the second attempt.

RIDER ERROR This is the most common reason for refusals/ run-outs. Indeed, it could be argued that rider error is the root cause of misunderstanding and that past errors may also contribute to a horse's disobedience. Any of the errors on the approach or at the jump, outlined earlier, may cause problems and it is very important once you start competing to learn to identify honestly and accurately any faults in your riding. Once you are in the ring, there is no instructor to help you and you only have limited chances to 'get it right'.

DISOBEDIENCE There is no doubt that there are times when some horses will refuse/run-out through sheer disobedience; that is, having been presented correctly and given every chance, they put in a 'dirty' stop. However, it is probably true to say that this happens a lot less than the times that horses go through with their effort despite the rider, so you must be very sure of your own innocence before blaming the horse.

Truly disobedient evasions tend to take the form of abrupt refusals and often occur in horses with a reputation for being generally ungenerous or dishonest. If there are no grounds for believing that their actions stem from some intermittent physical problem, then they should be dealt with firmly.

Preventing Evasions

Whatever the cause, a refusal/run-out still leaves the horse and rider the wrong side of the fence, so let us look at the steps which can be taken to redress this state of affairs:

1) If the cause was misunderstanding or rider error, it is inappropriate to punish the horse, although he may respond positively to a slap with the whip given as an encouragement when he is re-presented. After a refusal, you should not dither or flap about, but ride a fresh approach in a firm, controlled manner as promptly as possible. It is a mistake to go a long way from the fence and then return to steam at it in a flat-out gallop, as this will only alarm and unsettle the horse and is most unlikely to result in his jumping it. You should, rather, make a fairly short approach, starting in trot and then pushing on into canter for the last few strides. Bearing in mind that the horse has already declined the fence, you should ride the last strides strongly and give a firm aid to take-off, which may be reinforced by the voice and, perhaps, the whip.
2) If the horse has run out, it is, first of all, very important to stop him as soon as possible, so that he does not get the idea that he can just run away from the problem. For the same reason, it is helpful to turn him back against the direction of the run-out (for example, if he runs out to the left, turn him back to the right).

   Secondly, it should be borne in mind that if a horse has run out at an obstacle once, and attempts to do so a second time, he will almost certainly try to go the same way as before. To counteract this the rider should carry his whip on the 'run-out' side, and be prepared to use his leg on that side very strongly;

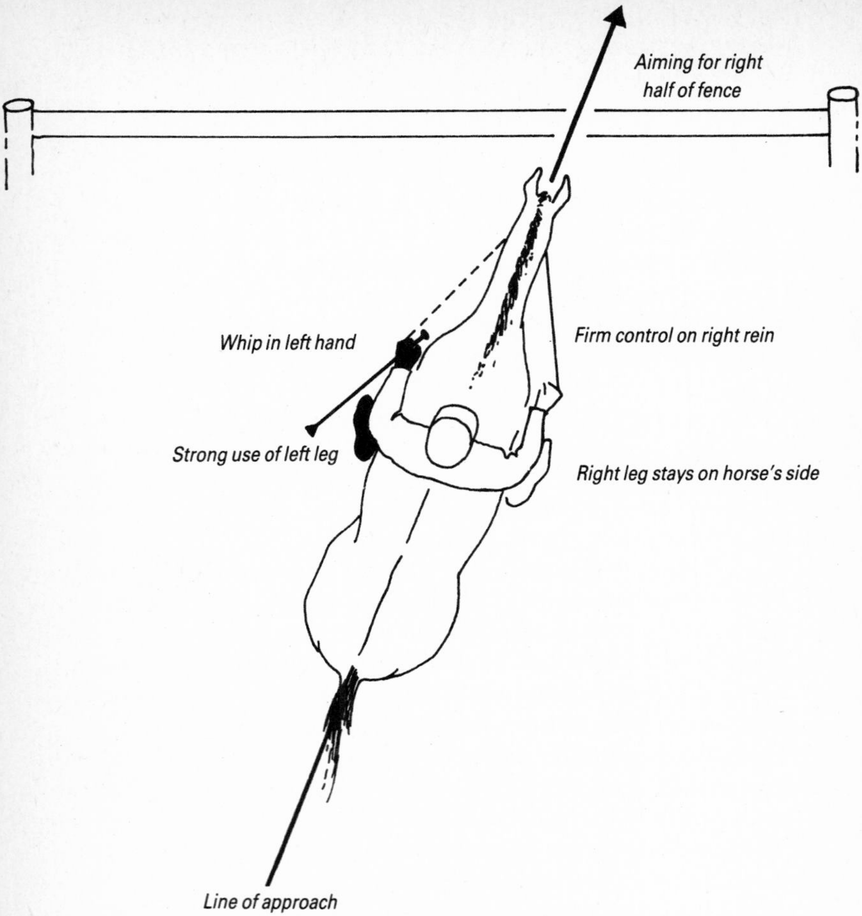

Remedial action after a run-out to the left – or corrective action anticipating a problem in that direction. If the problem were to the right, everything would, of course, be reversed he should also increase the contact on the opposite rein. Furthermore, it can be very useful to re-approach the fence at an angle from the side on which the horse has run out, aiming at the other half of the obstacle, so that, if the horse tries to turn in the direction he took previously he will find himself confronting the middle of the fence head-on, which may persuade him to take the line of least resistance and jump it.

3) The horse who has refused through sheer disobedience needs handling firmly, as he would if he displayed this trait in any other circumstances. Use of the whip may well be indicated, and this is an appropriate moment to consider how it should be employed when jumping.

Use of the Whip

In jumping, as in other areas of equitation, the whip may be used either for punishment or as an encouragement/stimulus. Its use is subject to various constraints:

a) Even if annoyed by the horse's behaviour, the rider should be in control of his temper when using the whip and should not use it excessively or improperly.

b) If used as punishment, it should be applied immediately the horse offers disobedience, so that the horse can make the association between his actions and the rider's response. For instance, if you intend to punish a horse for a 'dirty' refusal, you should do so while he is still stationary in front of the fence and not after you have ridden away from it.

c) The whip's use as an encouragement/stimulus must always be in conjunction with the natural aids. Furthermore, it follows that if you are seeking to encourage the horse to go forwards, your hands must be allowing him to do so.

If the horse is to be punished, the rider should take both reins in his free hand, maintaining a firm but not fierce contact, keep his legs on the horse and, reversing the whip from the 'carry' position, apply it firmly a couple of times to the horse's quarters (*not* his loins or stifle).

When used to reinforce the leg aids, the whip will usually be applied behind the rider's leg, as in flat work. It should be used the moment the rider feels or senses a loss of impulsion, especially if this occurs on the approach to a fence – there is no point in allowing the horse to come into a jump going slower and slower, and then hitting him when the position has become irretrievable.

Should the horse become very lazy or nappy, the whip can be used as for punishment, but in conjunction with strong leg aids and an 'allowing' hand.

The applications of the whip here described should not be attempted until the rider is confident of retaining his balance, and a correct rein contact, when jumping. There is a further application in which these criteria, especially the rein contact, are even more important; using the whip down the horse's shoulder. This is the only time, except for when using a long schooling whip on the flat, in which the whip hand remains holding the rein and, for this reason, some instructors are dubious about it. Nevertheless, when executed correctly, this application can work wonders with a horse who falters at the last moment and it is well worth describing.

There may be times when a horse which seems to be going to jump falters and half stops almost on the point of take-off. This may happen because he sees something he dislikes about the jump at the last instant, or because underfoot conditions cause him to reach the fence on a worse stride than expected. In these circumstances, he may need an instant stimulus to go through with his effort, not only to avoid penalties incurred by a stop, but also to prevent the risk of, for instance, putting his forefeet into a ditch, or between the lower rails of a fence.

A slap down the shoulder is the quickest response a rider can make in these circumstances; the whip remains in the 'carry' position and is applied by rotating the wrist and forearm away from the horse, and smartly back. The hand itself should not move out and away from the horse and it must certainly not move backwards. If you intend to use this technique, you should initially practise it dismounted, until you are sure that the only movement of wrist and forearm is a rotary one.

Finally on the subject of whips, you should be aware that most competition rules stipulate a maximum length of 0·76m (2·5ft), thus ruling out schooling whips, which are not, in any case, very suitable for jumping. You should, however, carry a whip which is capable of practical application if required, and avoid those ghastly short plastic jobs which, although cheap, are still a complete waste of money.

Losing Control

Riders often do not so much lose control as surrender it and this is especially true when we are thinking of inexperienced riders on horses which may become keen or cheeky, but which should not be mad, bad or dangerous.

Some of the causes and cures have been dealt with earlier and it should be borne in mind that when you are trying to ride round a course the accent should be on preventing loss of control, or at least regaining it rapidly.

In the show-jumping arena, loss of control should be fairly unlikely, since space is limited and the rider should have the horse going in a rounded outline on a relatively short stride. Points to avoid are 'throwing the reins at the horse' whilst in the air, and letting the horse run on because it 'seems to be going well'.

In cross-country competitions, things are rather different: there are wide open spaces, long runs between fences and the general tempo will be faster. The rider must come to terms with the fact that, if a horse does become excited in these circumstances, he will need considerably firmer handling than that normally applied in the dressage arena.

Many novice riders are reluctant to ride strongly for fear of damaging the horse's mouth and we have earlier studied the importance of not snatching or jabbing on the reins when jumping. However, whilst this sort of action is certainly to be avoided, there is little chance of injury to the horse resulting from the occasional necessity of taking up a strong contact, providing he is wearing a reasonably mild bit in good condition. It is chopping, jerking motions that cause damage, whereas a strong hold will cause a deadening of the mouth only if continued for long periods.

The basic method of checking an over-strong horse is, as described earlier, to allow the weight to come back behind the horse's centre of balance, with the rider's big back and leg muscles, rather than hands and arms, countering the horse's pull. The rider should keep his legs on the girth, rather than ram them far forwards and, retaining a steady contact on one rein, he should take and release the other in a measured manner, without snatching and without throwing away the contact. If it is necessary to persist, the action should be changed periodically to the other rein. When the horse responds by steadying and dropping his head, the rider should gently move his weight forward a little and soften the hand. If the horse maintains his improved rhythm, the problem is solved, but if he quickens again, the rider will have to repeat the process. This technique is a 'souped-up' version of the 'give-and-take' technique used on the flat to encourage a horse to flex at poll and jaw, and come 'on the bit'. However, whilst the rider's hands should not generally move backwards when 'giving and taking', they will do so to some extent in the circumstances described above, although not to the extent that the horse becomes seriously unbalanced or unable to keep a fairly straight course.

If a horse throws his head in the air and goes hollow-backed as he attempts to run off, the safest way of regaining control is, initially, to give him a little more rein and push him forward from the leg. Although this may encourage him to go faster, it is also very likely to bring his head down; once that has happened the reins can be shortened and the procedure described above adopted. While the horse has his head up, you should be sure to sit back, although you should not compound the problem by keeping a very short rein. It is dangerous to sit forward with a tight hold of the horse's head in these circumstances, because of the possibility of being dragged off forwards between the horse's forelegs. Points to avoid when trying to retain/regain control are:

1) Riding with over-long stirrups
2) A constant dead pull on the reins.
3) Snatching, jerking and sawing with the reins.
4) Getting in front of the centre of gravity. As with the process of jumping, it is important that in the 'poised' position your weight is not in front of the horse's centre of gravity.
5) Trying to hold a pulling horse with just hands and arms.
6) Taking your legs 'off' the horse.

To get further insight into the principles of controlling horses, it is useful to watch horse trials riders in the cross-country phase and jockeys going down to the start of races.

Finally, it should be borne in mind that, however much you are having to restrain a horse on the flat, if you intend to take a fence you must allow the horse to go forward at the jump. You cannot get away with fighting a horse right into and over a fence; you must give him an aid to jump and a chance to do so.

Falls

The topic of falls is rarely broached in instructional books, but the truth is that anyone who rides, let alone jumps, regularly is likely to have the occasional fall. In novice jumping, the vast majority of falls are of the rider only and occur when balance is lost beyond the point of return. The most common types of fall result from one of the following situations:

1) Horse refuses and rider goes over horse's head/shoulder.
2) Horse swerves suddenly to run out and rider keeps going straight.
3) Horse takes off a stride earlier or later than expected by rider.

If you apply the techniques described earlier in this book correctly, you should avoid the first two types of fall in most circumstances, since they stem from anticipating the jump. There is no reason why the rider who stays 'with' the horse and rides it decisively up to the moment of take-off should be unseated by a refusal/run-out unless it is *very* sudden and 'dirty'.

The third situation is not very likely to cause a fall once the rider has some degree of experience and can sense that there is something amiss with the approach. In the early stages, or if you are on an unfamiliar horse, it is usually safest to assume that if the horse is meeting a fence on a bad stride he will put in an extra, short one. As long as you sit well into the saddle and keep your legs on, he will probably take the fence in safe, if unspectacular, style. If he does 'stand off', you are at least in a secure position and can slip the reins to accommodate his extra effort. On the other hand, if you commit yourself to, and ride for, a 'long one' and don't get it, you can create problems for yourself and, possibly, the horse.

What happens, however, if you do have a fall, for whatever reason? Firstly, although it would be unrealistic to suggest that injuries never happen, they are pretty rare; you would be unfortunate to suffer much more than muddy breeches and the odd bruise. If you have time for thought on the way off, you should avoid the instinctive pushing out of a hand and arm to 'save yourself', because this can result in injury to wrist or collarbone.

Once off, you should, if possible, try to keep hold of the reins, since this may save you much chasing round fields and also prevent possible disruption of other competitors. If, however, there is a risk of being kicked, trodden on or dragged then you should let go.

Provided you are unhurt, and still in possession of your horse, your next step is simply to remount and finish the course, trying to avoid a repetition. If there is no real point in completing the round, you should still jump one more (straightforward) fence before retiring, so that you end on a positive note.

Should you be winded or shaken, you should give yourself time to recover fully before continuing, or you may risk further difficulties. If you do have the misfortune to fall badly, and have reason to believe that you have sustained injury, you should remain on the ground until qualified assistance arrives. Such assistance should be in attendance at any properly organised show and even an informal affair should have someone with first-aid training available.

If the horse falls, you should satisfy yourself that he has not been injured before continuing, asking for an opinion from an experienced person if necessary.

10 Safety Precautions

Having just looked at the less happy aspect of jumping, this is an appropriate time to think about safety. Riding is a sport which does contain an element of genuine risk, but there are certain causes of 'accidents' which are quite unnecessary, and there are also precautions which can prevent, or lessen, damage or injury.

If you ride at a reputable stable, many of these points should already be familiar, but it is alarming how often riders display ignorance of potential dangers, especially those involving tack.

Personal Attire

For riding in general, and jumping in particular, you should wear a hat which conforms to current British Standards Institute requirements. Furthermore, the hat should not have suffered a heavy blow, it should fit you properly and be correctly secured. It is best to buy your own from a reputable tack shop, who will advise on fit and adjustment. Borrowing an old, soft hat of obscure ancestry which does not fit and which is secured with a bit of elastic (or nothing), is, to put it mildly, a foolish risk.

Footwear should, ideally, be proper knee-length riding boots, be they rubber or leather. Jodphur boots or 'dealer' boots may suffice, but give no protection to the lower leg from the possible ravages of jump stands, brambles, gateposts, etc. Other forms of footwear are inadequate, or even dangerous, since they may increase the risk of the feet becoming caught in the stirrups.

It is a good idea to wear a decent pair of leather-palmed gloves, which will not only help you to maintain your hold on the reins in adverse conditions, but will also protect them from grazing in the event of a fall. Similarly, a long-sleeved garment will protect the arms; when show-jumping, this will normally be a jacket, but when riding cross-country in hunter trials or horse trials, it is safer to avoid the temptation to wear short sleeves, or roll the sleeves up.

If you have to wear spectacles when riding, it is worth getting a pair with robust frames and shatterproof lenses, which should be fairly large to prevent the wind from eddying around them into the eyes, which can cause severe watering. Ladies who wear earrings should remove them, since they can catch on branches and cause unpleasant injury.

Tack

Always check your tack before riding, but be doubly vigilant if you are going to jump. Check that the bit is correctly fitted and that all buckles and stud fastenings are secure and in a good state of repair. Similarly, check the stitching on reins and girth buckles, ensure that the girth is sufficiently tight (recheck before competing) and check the condition of the stirrup leathers. Ensure that the stirrups themselves are not cracked or twisted and are neither over-large nor too small for your feet. Also, be absolutely certain to check that the 'safety catches' on the stirrup bars are down. You must *always* ride with these catches down so that, if you do have the misfortune to come off with a foot caught in the stirrup, your weight will quickly drag the stirrup leather free from the saddle. (These catches, in fact, serve no useful purpose and the sooner they are re-designed with only the safety option, the better.)

It is a good idea to tie a loop knot in the reins around the buckle, so that, if the buckle becomes unfastened (it happens!), the reins are still joined by the knot. This is especially important if the reins are unduly long, since it helps prevent loops which can ensnare the rider's whip at a crucial moment, or, more seriously, his leg. I have witnessed an instance where a rider lost a stirrup and regained it, but in doing so, he put his foot through a loop in the reins – this is obviously potentially dangerous.

The old practice of providing neckstraps for riders starting to jump appears to be on the decline. A neckstrap is simply a stirrup leather or something similar fastened loosely round the base of the horse's neck, providing something (other than the reins) for a rider who has lost his balance to hang on to. Provision of neckstraps might alleviate the tendency for inexperienced riders to fling themselves forward and wrap their arms round the horse's neck when in difficulty. I have recently seen two riders get away with this, but it is a very dangerous practice, since it is extremely difficult to regain one's seat and control from such a position; if the horse keeps going and the rider does come off, it will probably be a case of slipping round the horse's neck and falling between his front feet.

More generally, you should be very wary of stables which habitually provide horses dressed up in a lot of gadgetry and also be cautious of the horses themselves. Horses for novice riders should be capable of going well in a simple snaffle bridle. However, they may wear breast girths or cruppers if their physique warrants it, and some establishments do like to use running martingales; basically because they are unsure of the positioning of their clients' hands. Beyond this, things start to look dubious; the horse who 'needs' fancy bits and nosebands more probably needs (re)schooling, and this is not the function of the novice who, after all, is a paying client.

General

It should be commonsense not to ride if you feel unwell, if you are suffering from an injury which may either affect your ability or be aggravated by a fall, or if you are taking medication which affects your concentration. Also, although I don't suggest that you should ride in a state of semi-starvation, it is unwise to ride on a full stomach, be it full of solids or liquids. This can be very uncomfortable and will certainly have an adverse effect if you are riding a competitive round. Furthermore, it may prove very messy and unpleasant if you fall off!

11 Looking Ahead

Having dwelt for a while on the darker aspects of jumping, I would like to conclude on a more positive note, by looking at what the keen novice may expect to get out of the sport.

Many riders start with no greater aspiration than to get round a novice course without looking completely foolish, but the bug soon bites and they get the urge to progress to greater things. Once, then, you have reached the stage where you can perform competently on a well-mannered horse, you should consider the following:

1) Try continually to improve your basic riding, concentrating as much on flat work as on jumping; try to ride every horse, and every movement, as well as possible.
2) Practise seeing a stride. Don't spend time just letting the horse arrive at the jump anyhow and scramble over – try to place him correctly and when you do come to a fence wrong, at least be aware of the fact and ride accordingly.
3) Practise control, balance and rhythm on turns, looking forward to the time when you will want to be competitive in timed jump-offs. (Once pupils have reached a reasonable stage, a good instructor will spend time teaching them to tackle fences met on short approaches off corners.)
4) Watch top riders closely, try to absorb the 'feel' of their riding and how they look in flight over different types of fence. It is best if you can actually be present, but television or film are useful media (especially helpful is video, with its playback facility). Watching with someone experienced is a good idea, since they may be able to explain why a rider tackles a fence in a particular way, or even why they get into difficulties. It will become apparent that the basic principles of jumping are very

much the same at all levels; on the rare occasions that famous riders make mistakes, the mistakes are likely to be the same as are seen at local shows.

5) If you are not fit already, then get yourself reasonably so. Competitive riding can be surprisingly demanding, even at a modest level, and the fitter you are, the more able you will be to control and assist the horse.

If you can demonstrate a lot of keenness, and a degree of competence, you may be surprised by the opportunities that come your way. There are some very helpful and generous stable owners around who may, once they know you and your riding ability, allow you to hire a suitable horse to take to local shows, and generally offer encouragement and assistance. It goes without saying that such attitudes should be responded to in the same spirit; you must be ready to help prepare the horse, clean tack, etc., and must always try to ride to the best of your ability. Furthermore, you should be grateful for the opportunity and experience regardless of whether you come home with a cup or just muddy breeches; apart from any other considerations, fluctuating fortunes are part and parcel of equestrian sport.

Looking further ahead, there are a surprising number of horse owners who, for various reasons, do not compete on their own horses. If you do not, or cannot, aspire to owning your own horse in the future, you may still be able to come to a happy arrangement with such a person and perhaps find yourself riding a very decent horse.

Go on, surprise yourself.